TO SERVE
AND PROTECT

Other books in THE CHRISTIAN AT WORK IN THE WORLD series:

Caretakers of Creation: Farmers Reflect on Their Faith and Work
by Patrick Slattery

Kindling the Spark: A Dialog with Christian Teachers on Their Work
by David Sorensen and Barbara DeGrote-Sorensen

Of Human Hands: A Reader in the Spirituality of Work
edited by Gregory F. Augustine Pierce

TO SERVE AND PROTECT

Law · Enforcement · Officers Reflect · on · Their Faith · and · Work

JUDITH A. KOWALSKI and
MAJ. DEAN J. COLLINS

AUGSBURG
Minneapolis

ACTA
Chicago

TO SERVE AND PROTECT
Law Enforcement Officers Reflect on Their Faith and Work

Published by Augsburg, 426 South Fifth Street, Box 1209, Minneapolis, MN 55440 and ACTA Publications, 4848 N. Clark St., Chicago, IL 60640.

Scripture quotations are from the New Revised Standard Version Bible, copyright © 1989 by the Division of Christian Education of the National Council of the Churches of Christ in the United States of America. Used with permission.

Cover art and design: Judy Swanson

Library of Congress Cataloging-in-Publication Data

To serve and protect : law enforcement officers reflect on their faith
  and work / [compiled by] Judith A. Kowalski and Dean J. Collins.
     p.   cm.—(The Christian at work in the world)
    Augsburg ISBN 0-8066-2613-5 (alk. paper)
    ACTA ISBN 0-87946-065-2
    1. Police—Religious life. 2. Christianity and law. 3. Vocation.
  4. Police—United States—Interviews.   I. Kowalski, Judith A.,
  1937– . II. Collins, Dean J., 1946– . III. Series.
  BV4596.P7T6   1992
  248.8'8—dc20   92-11544
                                                CIP

Manufactured in the U.S.A.   AF 9-2613

96   95   94   93   92   1   2   3   4   5   6   7   8   9   10

This book is dedicated to the
men and women who have
dedicated their lives to the
public by serving as law
enforcement officers.

•

"No one has greater love than
this, to lay down one's life for
one's friends."
(John 15:13)

• CONTENTS •

• PREFACE •

These are the personal stories of law enforcement officers and their spouses willing to reflect upon the interaction between police work and the Christian faith. This book is neither a scientific study of law enforcement, nor a technical book on spirituality. Rather, it presents interviews about the faith and work of particular people in their own words.

There are a number of ways to define spirituality. Perhaps the one that best describes the approach taken in this book is by Carolyn Osiek, who says spirituality is "the experience, reflection and articulation of the assumptions and consequences of religious faith as it is lived in a concrete situation." The concrete situation of law enforcement officers is a difficult, dangerous, and often violent one. The spirituality they discover there is, of necessity, different from that found in other professions. The religious faiths represented by these officers are varied, although spirituality certainly encompasses much more than denominational affiliation. The experience, reflection, and articulation found in these pages are primarily those of the officers or spouses themselves. Additional comment and analysis is offered by the authors at the end of each chapter and in the conclusion.

The process used in interviewing these men and women was to ask them to tell their story, noting anything remarkable about their work. They were asked to comment on the way their religious faith interacted with a career in law enforcement, and conversely how that career affected their spiritual lives and religious commitments.

As they point out, law enforcement officers live out many of the principles of healthy spirituality: helping others, seeking justice, protecting people from harm, upholding right, seeking truth, respecting the law, saving people from death, stopping violence, peacefully intervening in wrongful situations, and living on the edge of life and death.

On the other hand, they demonstrate that some of the job requirements of law enforcement may present unique challenges to developing a healthy spirituality. People don't call the police for good things. They call when something bad is happening. Police officers by their unique calling are enmeshed in pain, suffering, and evil. That's what makes their job so difficult. As one of our interviewees notes, they experience evil out of all proportion to its existence in the universe. This immersion in the evil side of life can sometimes take its toll on the souls and spirits of law enforcement officers.

How to resolve this conflict is the spiritual task of law enforcement officers. For Christians, law enforcement can be a ministry as well as a job. They need only to recognize that possibility and act upon it.

The opinions and comments of the authors are their own, and are not to be attributed to any other person, organization, or governmental agency.

Judith A. Kowalski, Ph.D.
*Deputy Inspector Dean J. Collins

---

*In the field of law enforcement, the rank of deputy inspector is equivalent to the rank of major.

• 1 •

JEROME STARKE

I Love *Coming to Work*

The greatest job in the world

Lieutenant Jerome Starke is the court administration lieutenant, Milwaukee Police Department, Milwaukee, Wisconsin. He is, as he puts it, in the twilight of his career. As he looks back over the years, we find him expressing in many ways the love he feels for his work, for his fellow officers, for the people he serves, and for his spiritual roots and formal education in the Catholic church. While love is the heart of religion and spirituality, we might not think of looking for it in a police station. Lieutenant Starke points out fellow officers who engage in the highest form of love, and he says "it is beautiful to watch" such professional officers at work.

I *love* coming to work! This is the greatest job in the world because of the built-in reinforcements it has. In spite of all the stress that officers go through, the positive reinforcements of arresting a burglar, a child molester, or a drunk driver are endless. Some psychologists have said there are certain things people desire in life. Besides security and recognition, they desire new experiences. There are people in high places in

11

corporations, even bank presidents, who would give their right arm to ride in a squad car for one night, just to enjoy the new experiences. Here, we deal with them every day. When an officer leaves the station at the beginning of a tour of duty, he or she has no idea what is going to happen in the next eight hours. That can be a very positive thing. It's an extremely interesting job. I will hate to leave it when I retire.

Until recently I was the day lieutenant at District 4, Milwaukee Police Department. The captain runs the district and I ran the shift. There are between forty-five and fifty-five people, sworn officers and civilians. I handled the daily activity there, including calls for police service and investigations. I oversaw the operations making sure the officers were doing the right thing the correct way and giving us a fair day's work. I relied on the officers to operate on their own but there are certain ways I could see if they were doing it. I recorded their activity. I looked at how many traffic citations and warning cards they issued. I checked whether they answered their police radio when they were called, and the way they handled investigations. I checked their reports, making sure they were neat, accurate, complete.

•

I respect the officers there. I remember when I was a young sergeant and lieutenant. The first thing I would ask was, "What would the detective bureau think if I did it this way?" I knew the right way to do it, but I always asked myself, "Is this going to be a career buster if I do it this way?" As I got older, I found out that I had the same ability as they did to make good decisions. Now I'm in a much more comfortable position to make decisions, and I make better decisions than I did back then. The officers I work with are also experienced. I trust their decisions.

The day-to-day decisions are the tough ones. When somebody's life or limb is dependent on your decision, you hope you make the right one. If a wife is afraid of her ex-husband, you could take a cavalier attitude toward it and say, "That's her problem," but in fact it's not her problem. It's our problem to protect her. But then, on the other hand, you have to decide if this is an overreaction on the part of the wife. So you have to make a judgment. But there are very few decisions I've made that I've ever regretted. I make them based on the information I have, what I know at the time.

The thing that would bother me most would be if one of my officers went out and got hurt or, God forbid, got killed because I've failed to convey some information to him or her. Those kinds of things always bother me. It might be a description of somebody wanted, for example, who might be carrying a gun. If an officer didn't get that information from me, and went out and met that person and got hurt, that would be pretty hard for me to handle.

•

Motivation, too, is part of this job—like it is for any manager, any supervisor. How do you motivate people? I learned a long time ago that police officers can only motivate themselves. What I can do is create a good working environment. That's how I help motivate my people. I worked with older officers at District 4. Day-shift officers are all 15- to 20-year veterans. I treat them with respect, make them feel important. They *are* important.

I want them to enjoy coming to work. We don't have a tough military attitude here, where everything is, "Yes, sir! No, sir!"—all rules and regulations. I want the officers feeling comfortable, feeling good when they leave the station. If they leave here with a negative attitude, that can be very dangerous. Of course there are times, like on any other job, when I have to climb on people because they are not doing their job right. But, even so, we can still create a good environment. And we do. Our people have good equipment and uniforms. Their working hours are good. The job isn't that tough. If we can integrate their goals with our goals, we will have a successful operation. I can help them understand that their position is very important, and it is. There is nothing wrong with being the best patrol officers they can be. You don't have to be a sergeant or a detective or a deputy inspector to be called a success in this job.

There are coppers out there that do the job extremely well, better than I could ever have done. They're satisfied with their work. That's all they want to do in life. They're happy people. They don't want the hassle of being a supervisor. They just want to go out and perform their job.

A lot of them say, "I want to help people," and some of that might sound corny, but they really mean it. Sometimes this can be a drawback, especially with the older officers. You'll find the older officers do not like to make arrests. They'd rather solve the problem. They'd rather stop a motorist and shake their finger and say, "Now, if you don't slow down you're going to kill yourself or somebody else, or your family is going to suffer." The officers will give them a big fifty-dollar lecture instead of a fifty-dollar citation, because they know that otherwise the driver is going to get hit with a money fine and maybe with an insurance rate hike.

The younger officer is looking for the arrest, "the pinch." That is the way they get ahead. The older officers, when they go to a family trouble call, want to solve the problem. Arrest is their *last* option. For the younger officers, that's their *first* option. Arrest them, throw them in jail, solve the problem. These older guys, they've lived. They know what life is all about. It is beautiful to watch. But it doesn't show up in the numbers column.

I'm real pleased with our group at District 4. They take their jobs very seriously, but they don't take themselves seriously. If one seems to look more important than the other, the other one lets him know pretty quick. So it is a fun place to work.

•

A high point in my career was working at District Number 5 in the inner city as a sergeant and lieutenant. I enjoyed that. There is more active Christian concern shown in an eight-hour shift in that district than some people ever show in a lifetime. There are officers putting their lives on the line every day. They are not just making arrests. Officers will bring in their old clothes and take them over to somebody's house and never say anything about it. You find out about it another way.

I remember an old streetlight over a wino sitting in a doorway. He had a nice clean shirt on. He told me he got it from an officer. What did Jesus say? "As you did it to the least of these my brethren, you did it to me"? These officers do that every day. There were a lot of people, really *good* people, who lived in that district. I've seen people come into that station who didn't have anything, but they were paying their parking fines and purchasing their parking permits. It was the last six bucks they had, but they wanted to obey the law. Those are the people to whom you don't mind extending yourself. Sure, there is a lot of crime in the inner city, but there are certainly a lot of victims, too.

If you want to become involved in Christian care and concern, that's the place to do it. More than you can handle! Some do it very quietly. I used to collect toys from the other coppers for the Milwaukee Boys Club. The coppers wouldn't use their own name. They just said, "Here." They didn't want anything in return. Benevolent love.

Some people say there is no such thing as benevolent love, love where there is no return, where I'm doing it just for you. Love for the sake of love is very rare, but you can find it. A mother's love for her child, that would be benevolent love. She wants nothing in return, just so the child is comfortable, happy, and fed. Nothing in return. You see that kind of love at District Number 5. The officers get nothing out of it, except a good feeling. They don't go around and say, "Hey, Sarge, guess what I did? I gave fifty bucks to the guy on the corner." But they do it.

•

At District Number 5, we had about fourteen squads. Of the fourteen, where do you suppose three of those squad cars were at five-thirty on a Sunday morning? They were in the back parking lot of St. Elizabeth's Church. The officers would say, "It's our lunch time, Sarge," but they were going to church. The inspector of detectives always went to that Mass. He would look around, look up in the choir loft, and see those coppers up there and never say a word. It was the quiet time at the district. If we needed them, we knew where they were. The reason I saw them there was because I went there, too. They knew I was there. Everybody looked the other way. It was nice to see that. It was third shift after a busy Saturday night. All the drunks are home, family troubles are over, the shootings are all done. It's the quiet time.

If you go to Gesu Church, you'll find the whole vice squad goes to Mass there together after work. The detectives, when they get off work, or just before they get off work, sneak over to Gesu for the "twelve-minute Mass." If something ever goes down at that time, you know where to get them. They're always at Gesu. The priests know they are all cops who are about to get off duty, because they have their radio turned on low, or in their ear. If they get a call, they have to run. They say, "That's our lunch hour." Instead of going out to some restaurant, they go to church. How are you going to fault it? Mass is a spiritual reinforcement.

But it shows you what values these guys have. And some of them need help after a bad night. They don't understand why God allowed this or that to happen. But it's my opinion

16

that God didn't allow it to happen. God *knew* it was going to happen. Some people might say, "God took my child." God didn't take that child. He knew it was going to happen, but free will and the natural order of things caused that incident. God didn't. He didn't *will* you to get hit by a car. Somebody else, either the guy driving the car or you, caused that to happen. God simply knew it was going to happen. So, in answer to the question, did God want that child raped or killed? No. He didn't will that at all. That's the way I resolve that question.

•

I'm a practicing Catholic. I was a seminarian for three years in high school. I went to a dance one night and met girls, and that ended the seminary idea. I graduated from St. John Cathedral High School, and then Marquette University.

Cathedral High School was an extension of a Catholic grade school to me. It was just something you went through and played football and such. Marquette was a little different. Of course, I went to Marquette on a different level. It took me ten years going to night school! The president said, "You don't want a diploma, you want a pension!" I was the longest-running student there.

I majored in psychology and minored in philosophy. I remember the courses in ethics and metaphysics and the philosophy of man. It brought everything into focus. It brought God into it. I remember the priest who taught in our ethics class. The first day he said, "How many people believe in God?" Everybody raised their hand. He said, "Well, I don't. I believe in Mickey Mouse. I'm going to show you that we are both right." What he wanted us to do is to arrive at the existence of God through our natural reason. All our lives we had been told by the theologians and the priests that God exists. He said, "Now, I want you to do it through natural reason, like Thomas Aquinas did in his *Summa Contra Gentiles*." He said we each have the power to realize the existence of God through our natural reason. We don't have to have anybody else tell us. He showed us how to realize, just through our common sense, that every mover has a prime mover, and every effect has a cause. Then, yes, you conclude there must be a God. That makes our faith much more solid. What if those priests were lying to me, or what if the sister wasn't right, you know? I proved to myself that they were right, through another avenue, through philosophy, natural reason.

I also got a much firmer grasp of what the Mass is about at Marquette. I had a whole semester on the Mass. We learned what the Mass meant, the gifts, Jewish tradition, the sacrifice of the lamb, and all that. When the professor explained the thing, I could understand it and could appreciate the Mass that much more.

I haven't really dropped out of church in my life. I wish there was more excitement, sometimes, like the Baptists have. They rouse you! They don't use the same old songs and clichés and humdrum homilies. I want to be moved! Did you ever hear a priest get up there and really hammer out a homily? You get every word of it. Most sermons are just dull.

I used to hear, "If you do this or that you're going to burn in hellfire for it." Now, I don't believe in hellfire anymore. No! The Jesuits explained it to me this way: Hell is being deprived of the beatific vision. That's hell. I don't think God is that kind of God to burn people in hellfire.

You know what I can remember when I was in grade school? The nun told this story. "Everybody was at Sunday Mass except Johnny, who went fishing. Johnny slipped on a rock and fell in the lake and drowned. He will burn in hell for eternity, because he didn't go to Mass." Ahhh! If only I could get hold of that nun today! That's religion based on fear. The Jesuits took care of all of that fear-based religion for me. Anytime I could get a Jesuit I would sign up for that course.

I also got *good* insights on law enforcement (at Marquette) from the Jesuits in the philosophy department. We had some nice talks about God's law versus human law. Do they ever conflict, do they ever cross? The priests said, "They can't cross. If they do, one of them is wrong." I've never seen a situation where human law contradicted God's law.

I believe most human laws are based on God's law in our country. I've never seen a real conflict between the two, but there may be the appearance of conflict. Abortion, for example, is one problem area. Yet I have no qualms about arresting an abortion demonstrator—or anti-abortion demonstrator—if they're violating the law. I never involve myself in what their cause is. I can't. I just ask myself, are they violating a law or denying somebody their rights? If they're doing that, then they're applying the Machiavellian principle that the end justifies the means. That's wrong.

•

I was just a young sergeant when I was going through the riots in 1967. It was four or five days before I got home. I was feeling pretty good about how we handled the situations we encountered but the violence, including the shooting, certainly had an effect on me. It was difficult, but I was also proud of myself. I recall one evening, my wife and I went out to see the musical *West Side Story*. Anna Maria Alberghetti was the lead singer. I was enjoying the play. But when it came to the part where Tony shot a gun, *bang!*, I gasped and had to leave the theater. That told me I *didn't* have control of myself. When that gun went off I just jumped up and couldn't breathe.

Comments by the Authors

The opinions and comments of the authors are their own, and are not to be attributed to any other person, organization, or governmental agency.

Two themes that are prominent in the Roman Catholic Church are love and unity. These are also themes that become evident in the story Lieutenant Starke tells of his life in the police department. Although he may not have been consciously trying to emulate the teachings of his church, they seem to have permeated his spirituality to the point that he does live them out. He speaks easily of love and the ways it is expressed in the police department. He speaks of his efforts to unify the personal goals of his officers with department goals and to unify department service with community needs. In that sense, he is an embodiment of the assumptions of his religious faith, a faith that serves others.

Although he makes light of it, Lieutenant Starke's ten years at Marquette University may have been instrumental in developing the healthy spirituality he displays at this point in his life. As we hear him tell his story, we see that the university was a place where he had access to highly skilled theologians on an ongoing basis. He took full advantage of that.

Since his college education took ten years, it proceeded alongside of his growing experience as a police officer, and not before he faced the real challenges of police work. Therefore, Lieutenant Starke had the opportunity to discuss with theologians some questions that he faced on the job as they arose in that context, such as the relationship between human law (which he enforced) and God's law (which he embraced). The university environment gave him a natural forum for high-level discussions about religion, which might not have taken place if he had had to seek out someone to discuss these issues with him. Without the university, he might not have discussed law enforcement questions in relation to religion at all. In building a healthy spirituality, it is necessary to reconcile religious principles with the everyday work done throughout a person's lifetime. Lieutenant Starke had the advantages of proximity to trained theologians and an academic program that created a forum for discussion. Others of us will need to create for ourselves situations in which such religious discussions are regular and natural.

Lieutenant Starke's discussions with the Jesuit faculty at Marquette University also allowed him to move beyond an immature faith into a mature relationship with God, one that he developed and owned himself. He now knows *what* he believes and *why* he believes it.

A person's spirituality is lived out in the context of work, leisure time, and home life, whether it is planned that way or not. It is best if a person has a healthy, mature spirituality to draw upon, because then the person's day-to-day actions reflect a loving, concerned, God-centered stance toward life and toward others.

Many of the people engaged in law enforcement careers will not have the advantages that Lieutenant Starke had, such as long-term access to highly skilled theologians, a worship schedule that coincides with police work schedules, and a police department that doesn't find fault with the pursuit of spiritual health. Officers are not always able to provide these things for themselves, because they are dependent on church officials, educational institutions, and workplace scheduling for the development of their spiritual health. It would be healthy for officers to be aggressive in seeking out religiously trained people with whom to discuss job-related questions as they arise at work, especially if those situations are a challenge to the officers' faith.

Officers also need to take the initiative in discussing with their church leaders the availability of worship at times when officers can attend. Sunday morning services might seem sufficient from the point of view of those who run churches, but many officers work at that time and are thus cut off from their religious community. In many cases, bringing up the problem might solve it. In other cases, the officer might have to seek out another place of worship that coincides with his or her schedule.

• 2 •

MARY VAN HAUTE

I Don't Want to Live with You Anymore
Marriage to an officer

Mary Van Haute is a teacher at the Northeast Wisconsin Technical College, Green Bay. She is married to Allen Van Haute, who has been in law enforcement for sixteen years. They have two children. Because of the strains placed upon their marriage by the challenges of police work, Mary has studied police marriages. Her story gives us a picture of what it is like to live with an officer and what the work of law enforcement does to the people who perform that work every day. Mary has taught at patrol officer in-service training as a spokesperson for Concerns of Police Survivors and the National Law Enforcement Officers Memorial. Mary is also the secretary for a congregation of the Evangelical Lutheran Church in America.

I am so grateful that my marriage has turned around for me, because I know about so many marriages that haven't improved. I was sitting through the wedding of a cop on November 13, and I thought, "Here goes another one." Just a week ago there was a couple who had split up. Good friends. Married seven years. Two kids. Of course he said it had nothing to do with the job. She said he never talks.

With so many divorces, you run out of people to look up to when you're losing hope. When you think, "I can't do it anymore," you look to other couples and think they've made it. "They're just like me. They've made it this far." But then you run out of resources because so many of these couples are splitting up. They have amicable relationships with their ex-spouses. They say, "I really like you, but I don't want to live with you anymore." That kind of relationship. It's not even that they're bitter. It's just that they gave up. Although that is happening in many marriages today, I think it is magnified in this career.

In our marriage, we have managed to solve some of the problems. Unfortunately, they were resolved the hard way.

•

The one thing that surprised me about living in this marriage is the loneliness. I'm terribly lonely. In our younger years, I would close the windows, the shades, the doors—even on a sunny Sunday afternoon—because I didn't want to know what other people were doing.

I hated the way people didn't understand. They would make idle remarks, like, "Where's your husband?" "What do you mean, he's working Christmas? I thought he did last year. Can't somebody else work this year?" You feel so isolated, because you are home alone on Saturday night, or holidays, or whatever. Or you leave a social event early because he has to go home and get in the shower and go to work for the midnight shift.

That loneliness, I think, was further exaggerated by the lack of understanding. If I would have had someone else there who I could even meet eye to eye with, who would say, "I know how you feel," I would have felt much better.

I went through such a gamut of feelings, including guilt. Some people would jam down my throat, "Just be happy he's got a job." Then I'd feel guilty. I wanted someone who would say, "It's OK to feel guilty. I feel guilty, too."

I would force Allen into making decisions. I would force thoughts into his head. That was so unnecessary, but I just didn't want to be alone anymore. I just didn't care to tackle the things I had to tackle alone. In forcing him to make those decisions, or forcing him to do some things, I played mind games. I made idle threats and locked him into a no-win situation. But somehow, through the grace of God, he was able to see that these actions of mine were only temporary, and that at some point through lots of prayer and understanding I would understand more about why he was doing what he was doing.

●

Added to the isolation is the public's lack of understanding. My own mother-in-law, after twelve years, finally understands a 5-2-5-3 schedule (work five days, off two, work five days, off three). It took twelve years! She would repeatedly ask, "How come you're not coming over? You haven't been home in three months." I say, "It's because we haven't had a weekend off in three months." She would say, "I can't understand that. Can't somebody else work this time?"

I don't think the people in the general public have any idea what the life-style or the job of law enforcement is really like. I would often feel guilty because people would say, "Just be happy he made it home safe," and things like that. That's not our perspective. I don't think about him in a dangerous situation when he leaves the house. I say, "Don't forget the laundry." Our life is focused, like everyone else's, in daily tasks. Whether Allen is leaving at quarter to eleven at night, or quarter to three in the afternoon, or at five in the morning, those are still our main concerns. I don't think about his danger or the threats to him. But the general public can make me feel guilty about my crying and whining over the weekend when I should be happy he's alive. The public's idea of his job comes from the media, which has not done a good job of telling the whole story. Television, movies, and news stories overdramatize and sensationalize the job. Well, a spouse just can't focus on danger. He or she would go crazy. And neither do the officers. We live our lives like everyone else, and it just so happens that the scheduling makes it difficult.

•

Eventually, people stop calling you. They don't want to understand your shift. They just know that the last four times they called, you couldn't make it. They get tired of it. They say, "Forget it. It's not worth it." You really lose your social circle.

I used to be very jealous of people who had routines like bowling every week. I felt that that was something you could bank on. I'm very jealous of neighbors who go out once a month to a movie or to dinner. Our weekends together—when we have a weekend off—are so regimented. Everything has got to go as planned, and we all sit and smile and say, "We'll really enjoy this weekend, because that's all we have. No fighting!" We could be madder than a hornet with each other, but "No fighting!" because this is our last Saturday for two months.

Leaving church on a Sunday afternoon, when everybody else was planning some fun activity with their family, I would be thinking about getting him to work. I was so jealous. What would it be like to be able to say, "What should we do this afternoon?" We never, *never* think that way because his scheduling makes it impossible.

My daughters always ask, "Who's off tomorrow?" In a case like this week, Allen will be off Wednesday, Thursday, Friday, and then I will be off on Saturday, Sunday. It's pretty likely that during the majority of my children's week a parent is home with them. So, "Who's off tomorrow?" is a typical evening question.

•

As for our lives of faith, I see a big difference between spirituality and religion. I was raised in the Catholic church, and Allen attended the Lutheran church where we are now members. When we married I started attending church with Allen. Once our children were born, we decided we appreciated the experiences we were having together in the Lutheran church. I began teaching Sunday school there, and singing in the choir and volunteering for other tasks. The pastor finally approached me and said, "Before I ask you to be church secretary, would you officially become a Lutheran?" So I went through the training with him and became a member.

I joined our congregation because of what it fulfills for me socially and spiritually, and for the ministry that is going on there. That is so important to me. I think I could have chosen any church to accomplish these things, but it just happens that this is where it occurs for our family. As far as a person's spirituality goes, however, that comes from within.

I always did believe that marriage takes three and that Christ must be an *active* partner in it, not just a passive partner. I saw this being put to the test over the years. I think if Allen did not have the faith he had, we probably wouldn't have made it. My own faith was tested, and I took advantage of it. I said, "I just can't do it on my own. I surrender."

•

I had become focused only on myself in our relationship. I was frustrated with being alone. I was frustrated with not having a normal life-style. I wanted *out*. Or, I wanted *him* to get out. I was giving up and just wanted things better for myself. But Allen had the ability to say, "This is just something she's going through. I'll do my best." And he did. He tried. He applied for work at other places. He looked into other careers. But he eventually stayed in law enforcement. If he wasn't as strong as he was, our marriage would have fallen apart.

I think the only thing that snapped me out of it was coming to the point where I realized that *I* had to change. When we were married seven years an officer was shot and killed in our area. There were so many parallels with our own lives that I really believe it set me straight. It may sound so corny to say, "There but for the grace of God go I," but the situations with that officer's family and ours were so close, it made me appreciate life in general and become more aware of what was going on around me. I decided, "I'm putting so much energy into this self-focus that if I took that same amount of energy and put it into healing this relationship and to restoring my faith, I would be rewarded a hundredfold. If I could just get out of this self-centeredness." That event seemed like divine intervention.

•

Earlier in our marriage we had sought counseling for a year, but it was very superficial. The counselor wasn't able to realize what we were going through. She just didn't know our life-style. I give her a lot of credit—she was patient with us—but I don't think the counseling sessions ever penetrated the surface.

She spoke about opening channels of communication. My heavens! If anyone knew how to communicate, it was us, because we didn't have time to waste. We didn't have time for ambiguity or moodiness or pouting. I just wanted to throw my hands up in disgust and say, "You don't understand! We are *effective, efficient* communicators!"

We don't take things lightly. We have so much to do that we have to get it done. For example, Allen wakes up at five o'clock in the afternoon and gets in the shower at ten, and those five hours are my only time with him. That includes a meal. That includes time with the children. You bet we fight effectively! There are no kid gloves around here! I found that counselors just didn't understand. They didn't have the concept of what it really is like to be married to a cop, and what the true hang-ups were in our relationship.

It was the death of that officer and the effect on his family that intervened in our marriage. I knew that I couldn't resort to a support system that was "generic," so I put my energy into finding out what support groups existed for police families. I found there were none. I was on my own, but I found Allen again. I found a lot of my prayers being answered, though not the way I hoped them to be.

I changed because I had to change. I used to be so hung up on the superficial things that constituted Allen's job—the hours, the schedule, the overtime, the inability to give him a call at work. I'd watch him get ready for work and I'd be full of hate because of the way those things imposed on my life. Now that I know more about the people who have dedicated themselves to his career, I view those obstacles of scheduling and so forth as thorns in a rosebush. Knowing more about the career of law enforcement, I now know more about my husband and what compels him to be part of that camaraderie. I hope that I can continue to nurture that knowledge and forever put behind me the superficial obstacles.

We've been married twelve years, and as I look back I really believe there was divine intervention in our marriage. Someone was watching carefully, and Allen's faith helped everything turn out well.

•

Maybe if I had been better informed about law enforcement it would have helped make those early years easier. For example, I would like someone to have told me, "Hey, you are going to spend some time alone." I would have liked some answers to my questions. "What's a 5-2-5-3, for heaven's sake?"

In our early years, I would go sometimes to the day-care center to pick up our kids, and they were not there. Then I would remember Allen was off that day and had picked them up. It's routine now. Our family knows a Friday on the calendar is not a Friday for us. That's the life-style I wish I would have had more information about, and I wish I would have had more people around me with similar experiences. I thought I was the only one who was struggling. I thought I was going crazy.

The other cop families I know who have successful marriages often have their families living close to them. I think that makes a difference. Their Christmas Eve might be interrupted by their husband not being there, but they still have a Christmas Eve. They have other family members in town. Christmas wouldn't be that bad, I think, if you could run over to your mother's place. I had that choice, I suppose. I could have packed up and traveled a hundred miles and spent the time with my parents. But that wasn't my preference either. I wanted to be with Allen. Going to my mother didn't solve the problem. Think how unfair that would be for him to come home to an empty house on a holiday.

•

For the lows that we've had, there are also the highs; such as Allen sitting in front of a first-grade class with his daughter for show-and-tell. As his family, we know that what compels him to do the job he does is his basic goodness. He's kind. He's generous. He's forgiving. He's open-minded. His personality could be seen so negatively in terms of law enforcement, but it is a real positive.

I look back now and see that his schedule and working conditions were very advantageous to our family because he was with the kids. When they were real young, when our first baby was born, Allen was still on nights. But for the majority of their upbringing he was there with them. That's something I always try to accent when I write an article or speak to officers and their families. You really can look back and say it wasn't all that bad. And it *isn't* all that bad. It's just that you have to look for the positive things, and you have to truly appreciate them. I think the kids do. Their dad is so much a part of their life. I think that's very different from so many families today.

Just within the last month, for example, Allen was on a field trip with first-graders. We didn't make much of it, because he's certainly done that before. But the teacher actually pointed out to the class that they had a dad along. Allen didn't appreciate that, because to our children it was no big deal to have their dad along. He told the teacher, "Well, this is the way it has always been in our house. This is very normal for us."

In situations like that, I realize how fortunate we are that the children's father is so much a part of their lives. They don't call for Mom if they need a drink in the middle of the night. It's always Dad. That must be a sign of how important he is in their lives. Allison, our youngest, the first-grader, brought him for show-and-tell two weeks ago. He wore his uniform. He took them all out to the police car. She got to sit in the chair next to him in front of the room. He told me that at one point he looked at her, and she had such a forlorn look on her face. He put his arm around her and said, "Are you OK?" She started crying and said, "I'm so happy!" She was so proud to have him there.

•

I have learned to be more supportive. However, when Allen went out to Washington, D.C., to take part in the memorial service for officers who were killed during the year, that support was tested.

The day he came back from Washington, I will never, ever, forget. He was supposed to be back in the evening. Instead, as I was getting ready for work that morning, the phone rang. He said, "We're ahead of schedule. The bus will be at the station at ten-thirty. Can you pick me up?" I said, "Well, you know I am teaching a class. I can't." He said, "Would you *please* pick me up?" I said, "I'll do what I can. I've got a class." He said, "Please. *Pick me up!*"

I caught the sense of urgency in his voice. When I got to the station he was still unloading his stuff from the bus. I could tell again, just by the expression on his face, that I should stay clear of him. I waited in the car and I opened the trunk with the lever under the dash. He threw his things in without a word. He got in the car and didn't say a word. Finally, a tearful "Hello" came through a long embrace. We got home and he said to me, "Please hurry back."

I finished my class and when I got home he was still sitting at the kitchen table. He said, "I just want you to be here with me. I can't tell you about it now. I'm going to tell you. I plan to tell you, but I just can't talk about it now." He just wanted me to *be* there with him.

•

It took about two weeks before, bit by bit, things came out about what he experienced in Washington at the memorial service—escorting a widow at the service and getting to know firsthand about the tragedies of line-of-duty death. To this day, we don't talk about his experience a lot, but I know he has a bond with the particular widow he escorted that day which is sacred. It's almost as though no one else would understand. Even within the realms of police work, nobody's going to understand the bond between him and that widow. He was the one who escorted her to the memorial service. She collapsed into his arms. They were both overwhelmed by the experience.

Allen went to Washington to learn more and to show respect. But because his department had never lost an officer, he took some ribbing. People would ask me how I felt about him spending a weekend in Washington with all those single women. They'd ask me about it, but it wasn't worth trying to explain anything to them.

I know that the care and concern and whatever virtues Allen has that compelled him to be at that service are also what holds us together. It's what knits our family together. All the qualities that he gave to that survivor, I feel good about. I feel great knowing he will provide and care and continue to provide and care for people all his life in that way. Others actually had little perception of his motives. Some couldn't see the reason why he went or what his impetus was for being involved.

Allen came home from that event rolling with statistics. Things that I knew, but it was a chance to repeat them to each other. An officer dies in this country once every fifty-seven hours. He said to me, "We all knew the number." But, he said, they had to line up in a special area if they were escorting a spouse. "We waited in this roped-off area, and then the buses of survivors pulled up. I started to count them. I got to ten, then twelve, fifteen, sixteen . . . Buses *loaded* with survivors. All of a sudden the number, 156, the number killed in 1987, which you can just roll off your tongue, becomes real people, and the family members and the co-workers left behind are multiplied far beyond that number. And for what? Because these officers were doing their job! They were just doing their job."

Some officers will not participate in that annual memorial service in Washington, or even acknowledge it. I know from working with cops that this is true. That's crossing a line into a gray area they don't want to deal with. Death becomes too real. *Too* real. You don't want to think about it.

•

When a department loses an officer, the phones keep ringing, the shifts keep rolling, roll call continues. I sometimes chuckle when I see an ad in the newspaper that says, "Because of the death of so-and-so, the store or business will be closed." I think, "That's the way it should be!" But in the police department, the phones keep ringing and the place doesn't close down. But when does the slain officer's partner get a chance to break down and cry? When does everyone who worked with him have a chance to grieve? They don't, except maybe at a memorial service like the one held in D.C. and possibly at a C.O.P.S. (Concerns of Police Survivors) workshop, which does include officers as members and spokespersons. At least they have time to talk about their loss, to break down, and to publicly affirm that they are grieving.

•

During his daily routine, I can often tell whether Allen's day has been good, bad, or indifferent. He's the type of person that throws himself into an unrelated task to get over something. That's my way of knowing it hasn't been a good day. I'll come home and the fridge is pulled away from the wall, and he's scrubbing the floor. So I say, "OK? You want to talk about this?"

One day last winter, I watched him shovel snow while I was getting supper ready. I thought, "He's been out there a long time. What is he doing?" He would clear that driveway again as soon as enough snow came down to shovel. The paper had come late that night, too, because of all the snow. I finally got the paper and saw that was the day a twenty-five-year-old Dallas police officer had been shot and killed in public. He was shot to death on a street corner while a crowd gathered. That's what was bothering Allen.

It then took—and I think it will always take—my initiative to find out what's been going on in his day. I can open the door a little bit and tell him, "Maybe I don't completely understand, but I have an idea of what is bothering you." If I don't take that initiative, he won't share it with me. I don't think it's because he doesn't want to, I think it's because he doesn't know where to begin or how to initiate it. He will say, "It was a terrible day." Or, "It's been really busy." When he's working a lot of overtime, the stress is more obvious.

At those times when he does share with me, he always asks permission. He's very courteous about that. He'll say, "I don't know if you want to know, but. . . ." And then it is up to my discretion. I usually say, "Really, it's no problem," even though it may be something that actually makes me physically ill. I say, "God! I couldn't do that!" That may be the extent of my response.

We do get into some detail, without mentioning names or addresses or anything like that. But I know, from my training in stress disorders and in dealing with stress, that the moment when he experienced that thing—whatever it was—his system shut down, and he dealt with it matter-of-factly in order to do his job effectively. But, at some other point, he has to feel the blood that ran through his hands. He knew he couldn't take the time to feel it then, he could only do what he had to do and not feel, not taste, not hear, not smell, while everything was going on around him. But, eventually, he has to deal with it. That may happen by relating it to me.

Allen uses lots of expressions such as, "It was like . . .," "It was just like . . .," "I felt this. . . ." I'm tuned in to those words, knowing he's releasing something, handling it, coping. He spoke one time about holding a kid's head that was either impaled or projected out of a car window. (He was the first one on the scene.) All he could do was hold this kid's head up while the rescue squads were called. He just kept talking to the boy and watched him turn grayer and grayer as he was dying. When the rescue squad got there, Allen cleaned up the debris, got in his car, and continued working. When did he to have a chance to deal with that child's terrible death? Not on the job. He needed to be given the opportunity to deal with it at home.

I remember another time he came home very late for his dinner break. It must have been close to nine, ten o'clock at night. I thought, "Why bother coming home now?" He walked through the door, went to the bedroom to hang up his gun belt (he always kept it in a locked closet), and didn't come back out of the bedroom. I finally went in there and found him sprawled across the bed. He told me a little six-year-old boy had been pulled from the river. It was like, "I can cry about it now," and he did cry about it. And then he said, "I have to go," and he went back to work.

Later he started to tell me bits and pieces of the incident. He said the little boy's arms hung like a dishrag as he was pulled from the water. He would use terms that were so vivid and so clear, and I knew he needed to do that—whether I wanted to hear it or not. He needed someone to listen to him tell exactly what happened.

My choice would be never to hear the details. I'm very comfortable in my naive little society, which "knows" that everybody loves their children and doesn't let them wander, in which no one abuses drugs or alcohol. But, instead of cursing the fact that my husband forces another social reality upon me, I need to appreciate that he does so, because I know many officers don't talk with their spouses about their work. I have to see that this is a gift I was given—to be able to hear him talk about these things.

Our dialog is usually pretty selective. We may not have a lot of time with our schedules, but we make time. It may be in bed, and it may end with some form of confirming our closeness. I would say that it's always a very intimate moment. It doesn't just abruptly come and go.

The one thing Allen has told me, which I'm surprised about and need to give myself more credit for, is that it is easy to talk to me because I make an effort to understand the police system. I don't ever want to know all there is to know about police work. I have the highest respect for police officers, but I have no desire, in any way, shape, or form, to enter the career. But I need to know enough about the penal and judicial systems, to use the lingo that he is comfortable with, without saying, "I want to be one of the guys."

•

Our Lutheran pastor has helped us a lot. He has helped us as a couple, and I don't think I could measure the way he has helped Allen. They have each other. They both work in confidential careers where no names can be mentioned. They each suppress the stressful incidents they've dealt with because legally they can't talk about them. So when Allen and the pastor spend a day putting in eighteen holes at the golf course together, just the two of them, I don't think there is any amount of therapy or counseling or money that could buy what goes on in a day like that. Allen says, "I can let my guard down completely, and so can he, and yet it's totally confidential."

•

I've often asked Allen, "Do you ever pray on the job? Do you pray for someone when you are with them?" "Yes, of course," he says. As a way of talking about that, he'll put it in a humorous light. He told me about a time, for example, when he was wrestling with a huge person and tumbling down a flight of stairs. He said, "The only thing that came to mind was the Lord's Prayer. It wasn't that I was directly asking for help. I just remember saying the Lord's Prayer." He tells this as a humorous situation. It's his way of saying, "Yes, I pray, but don't let anybody know."

We have an annual Law Day service on May 1 when I can stand next to him and sing and pray when he is in uniform. That's mixing a lot of boundaries. Everybody comes to church in uniform, and it's their way of making a proclamation. The prayer service that we have is the officers' way to pray for strength and endurance, and for the rest of us to tell them that you can be a Christian *and* enforce the law. You don't have to choose one or the other. You *are* doing God's work.

Comments by the Authors

The social isolation that Mary Van Haute describes is almost inevitable for law enforcement families. Only cops can understand each other's lives, because they experience life and death in a unique way. They share a special knowledge: the sordid secrets of society. They rarely share those secrets with anyone. This, plus the scheduling, is why cops socialize mainly with other police families. Yet that isolation may give them a distorted view of society, leading them to think that the whole world is filled with the sordidness they encounter every day.

Healthy interaction with average people is necessary to maintain spiritual and mental health. The support and stability of a faith community is very important and can fill that role, as the Van Hautes clearly illustrate.

The relationship between Officer Allen Van Haute and his pastor is worthy of imitation (although not all pastors and parish members play golf together). Their experience points to the positive value of having a time and a place where an officer can talk confidentially with a theologically trained person. If the officer had to arrange a formal counseling session with the pastor, such discussions probably wouldn't happen very often. To include such a discussion along with other healthy pursuits, however, such as golfing or fishing, helps to relax both body and soul. Mary Van Haute is impressed by the blend of ministry and friendship that their pastor displays. It might also be pointed out that Officer Allen Van Haute shows those same traits in his work with the public and with his pastor. It is likely that the pastor needs those confidential conversations with Van Haute just as much as Van Haute does. Both need the tremendous release that comes with trusted friendship.

The description Mary gives of her growth from a self-centered and lonely person to a sympathetic listener is encouraging. She holds up hope for all young couples faced with the demands of law enforcement careers. Her listening to Allen when he is ready to talk and her acceptance of his experiences are inspiring. It takes a person with a big heart and loving soul to understand the kinds of situations that an officer faces. Mary not only educated herself in order to understand the police culture better, but she also "put in a sacred place" the special experience that Allen had at an officer's memorial service. Her respect for him and his feelings shows a mature spirituality that she has worked hard to achieve. Despite some disappointing experiences with a counselor, and the discouragement of increasing divorce among their friends, they both kept working at their relationship. It has paid off. Relationships are never easy, and police marriages add complexities that other marriages may not have to face.

Mary mentions Allen's prayer life and comments that he makes light of it, although he does pray in the course of his day at work. He recounts that one time when his life was in danger, he started saying the Lord's Prayer. Prayer is such an important part of what an officer can give to the citizens he or she serves. It can be done silently, but it is an effective and caring way to approach a crisis situation. Prayers in the car on the way to an accident, prayers over a dying person, prayers in private to develop a mature relationship with God, are all important components of a healthy spirituality.

"Macho" cops might scoff at the idea that their fellow officers are saying prayers, but they would not scoff at the serene officer who does not fall apart in the face of danger. Prayer is a way of developing the mature spirituality that is the foundation of strength and courage. We do not always spend time developing a mature prayer life. Sometimes we never grow beyond the little rhymes we learned as children. Officers who wish to grow spiritually, however, would do well to develop a working relationship with God, one in which honest, spontaneous prayer is natural.

Ministry within law enforcement involves more than prayers, although they are important, whether they are silent and private, ceremonial and public, or breathed by an officer over a dying citizen. The ministry of law enforcement itself is doing God's work. The book of Romans, chapter 13, tells of the role of public officials—including, and especially, law enforcement officers. "Let every person be subject to the governing authorities; for there is no authority except from God, and those authorities that exist have been instituted by God. Therefore whoever resists authority resists what God has appointed, and those who resist will incur judgment. For rulers are not a terror to good conduct, but to bad. Do you wish to have no fear of the authority? Then do what is good, and you will receive its approval; for it is God's servant for your good. But if you do what is wrong, you should be afraid, for the authority does not bear the sword in vain! It is the servant of God to execute wrath on the wrongdoer. Therefore one must be subject, not only because of wrath but also because of conscience" (Rom. 13:1-5). The very work of law enforcement itself is the work of God. There is no need to spiritualize it in any way.

•3•

THOMAS WINSLOW

I'd Fire the Officer That Gets Help

Personal and institutional denial

Thomas Winslow served in the State Fair Park Police Department, West Allis, Wisconsin, for twenty years before joining the Milwaukee Psychiatric Hospital as coordinator of the Professional Program, McBride Center. He rose from a part-time officer to chief in six years. His story gives hope for both departments and individuals who want to honestly find alternatives to substance abuse. We learn from his story how Winslow straightened out his life and his spirituality at about the same time.

There are really three parallel tracks we have to consider if you want to look at Tom Winslow as a person. One of them is the law enforcement career and what happens there. Then my religious focus, if any. And also my alcoholism. They are all part of a whole fabric. You can't eliminate one from the other, but I'm not so sure I fully understand how they interplay, either.

I had always been interested in law enforcement. I'm not sure why. When I was a kid I wanted to go to the Naval

Academy, but rheumatic fever knocked out any chance of that. After my wife and I were married, I wanted to go into law enforcement. I talked to Peg about it, but she was opposed to my working for the city of Milwaukee Police Department, which she perceived to be more dangerous than other municipalities in the area.

By 1968 I was disgusted selling life insurance and not making any money. One Sunday I picked up the newspaper and there were only two ads for police officers. One was for the city of Milwaukee, and the other was for a job with the Wisconsin State Fair Park. I called the Fair Park and asked them if I could apply, and they said "Yes. Come down this afternoon." I went down and applied. Within a week they had hired me as a part-time police officer, making me an employee of the state of Wisconsin. I began the process of working toward a full-time civil service position with them.

I'd had one semester of college full-time and had been taking some courses part time, so I had completed about a year and a half of college. In 1968 there weren't a lot of people who had any college applying for law enforcement jobs, so they were thrilled to have me apply.

•

I went to work with real vigor as a part-time officer, then got an appointment to a full-time position in August of 1968. In 1969, a deputy inspector of the city of Milwaukee Police Department retired there and came to the Wisconsin State Fair Park as chief of police. The new chief realized that none of the officers had any significant training. In those days it wasn't required by state or federal regulations as it is today. That October I was sent to the Milwaukee Police Academy for fifteen weeks, and I graduated at the top of my class. I don't attribute that to my being any smarter than anyone else, but I had been on the job about eighteen months when I went to school, so I wanted to go to school to learn what I needed, while the other guys in my class just wanted to get out on the streets as soon as possible. I was willing to study, but many of them weren't.

It turned out that I was employed at the right time. In 1970 the state of Wisconsin decided it was going to close State Fair Park, and they laid off most of the employees. I delayed taking a transfer to another state agency because I wanted to write a promotional exam for the justice department. By the time the state reversed its decision and decided to rebuild State Fair Park, I was the senior officer left in the police department. When the police chief became the acting director of the park, I became the acting police chief. I was in the right place at the right time, but I was also too young and too immature for the job.

•

Regarding my religious life, I was raised in the Episcopal church. I sang in the boys' choir at St. James, Milwaukee, and became an acolyte at a relatively early age. My whole spirituality, until recently, was wrapped up in the same kind of organizational mentality that served me well in law enforcement. If I was going to be an acolyte, I would serve Mass exquisitely. I would make sure everything was in the right place and would be very uneasy if I made any mistakes. I became very wrapped up in liturgical things as opposed to anything truly spiritual. The church taught me how to say prayers, but I learned how to pray later in Alcoholics Anonymous.

My wife and I were active in the Episcopal church when we got married in 1964. We remained active for several years. In 1968 Peg was in a choir at St. James. One night when I was late picking her up after choir practice, somebody broke into the building and beat her severely, almost killing her. To escape, she jumped out a window of the church into the parking lot.

It is interesting, in retrospect, that six weeks later I joined a police department. I've often wondered if it was a reaction to my wife's beating. I had always been interested in law enforcement and had growing dissatisfaction with insurance sales, but it's probably more than coincidental.

After that incident with my wife, and with some growing dissatisfaction with church politics on my part, it was relatively easy while working weekends as a cop to say, "I just can't be active in church anymore." We drifted away from the church—not because the church didn't have the answers that I was looking for, but as a matter of convenience. There were only so many things I could do, and I was enamored of this new life in law enforcement. Church just faded into the background. It was not a conscious effort. We continued to attend only at Christmas and Easter.

•

I started drinking when I was eighteen, though not heavily at first. I recall saying I wouldn't become an alcoholic because I became too sick when I drank. It never occurred to me that if you get sick when you drink, you should stop drinking. That logic escaped me.

In retrospect, I see that from the beginning I drank for effect. I felt inadequate. Drinking allowed me to feel better about myself, to escape from the things that I found too painful.

When I was working the midnight-to-eight shift, I had a great deal of difficulty sleeping during the day. I'd have a couple of drinks so I could get to sleep. Luckily I only had to work that shift for thirteen months. Somebody else left our department, and I went to the four-to-midnight shift.

On the four-to-midnight shift, of course, it was more socially acceptable to drink because the guys would go out after work. I suspect that a big difference between myself and others was that they quit after having a beer or two, but I would continue to drink at home. My wife was working, so she was always in bed by the time I got home. I would sit up, watch a late movie, have a pizza, and drink.

•

During this period in my life, I was also experiencing a growing inability to cope. I didn't perceive this as related to my alcoholism, but in retrospect it was. My job at State Fair Park was not all that dangerous. The perception by other law enforcement officers—that is, my perception of their perception—was that I was kind of a second-class officer. I had difficulty dealing with that idea, but, because of my own feeling of inadequacy, I didn't apply to a more prestigious police department. I set out half-consciously to prove that I was the "best of the second-best." If I was going to work in a small police department, I was going to prove that I was better than anyone else who did that.

I graduated from the police academy at the top of my class. I'm sure that a lot of that was a response to wanting to be the best. I immediately started taking courses in police science at the Milwaukee Area Technical College, although it took me a good ten years to complete an associate degree. I began doing in-service training and organizing of our police department. I rapidly rose from a patrolman, skipped sergeant and went to lieutenant, then captain, acting chief, and chief all within six years.

I became the chief of police at State Fair Park in 1974. I was twenty-nine years old when I became acting chief, and thirty when I became the chief. Although I had all these promotions validating me and telling me that I was doing well, inside I felt very inadequate. I continued to use alcohol as a way of dealing with that. I couldn't have explained it at the time, but eleven years into my recovery I have now begun to understand it.

At the age of twenty-nine I went to my doctor and said I thought I had a problem with alcohol. He told me that I was

45

suffering from stress as a result of my job in law enforcement and that what I needed to do was try to relax. He started me on a long list of prescribed medication, which taught me only that when I took medication I wouldn't have to drink as much.

•

I don't believe law enforcement caused my problems. Had I still been selling insurance I would have developed them also. Part of what happens in law enforcement, though, is a mind-set of what I call institutional denial. In chemical dependency circles we talk about individual denial. We arrange things to support the fact that we don't want to believe we are alcoholics, which makes it easier for alcoholics to remain alcoholics and not be challenged by their superiors to change their behavior. I believe such denial exists at all levels, however: individual, institutional, and societal.

In law enforcement, we are supposed to be what is described by Morton Bard of City University of New York as "human problem solvers." Human problem solvers are supposed to solve people's problems, not *have* problems themselves. So there is a bias developed within law enforcement that law enforcement professionals are not going to have problems.

That's reinforced by the way we codify our system and call it procedures and rules. Let me give you an example. There is a vast difference between saying, "It is inappropriate for a police officer to be intoxicated on duty," and "It is improper for a police officer to be an alcoholic." Unfortunately what has happened in many police departments is that the two have become synonymous.

The law enforcement system does a number of things. First, it denies that the problem exists. We develop rules against drinking on duty, and yet we create assignments in which part of your assignment is to drink while you are on duty. Undercover officers do that all the time. That's the nature of the job. I'm not saying it's wrong. What I'm saying is that in itself such a practice creates some conflict between what is and what is not appropriate behavior. Police departments have traditionally not had an understanding that chemical dependency is a disease process. Therefore they take a law enforcement approach and make it *criminal*. The police officers who have problems are perceived as bad police officers.

Police departments also assign people to places where it is difficult for them to remain emotionally stable and expect them to remain untouched by that. Such assignments include working in a high crime rate area in the inner city or in an undercover assignment for years. Sometimes cops in those situations don't have an opportunity to bond on the job with anyone that's healthy, yet we expect them to be unsullied, because they've sworn to uphold the law. It is as if we think we can legislate emotions and feelings. We have built a law enforcement system in which it is inappropriate—on an official level—to be sick.

Second, we know that a "blue code" of mutual protection exists. Police officers form a fellowship because officers perceive the world to be "them against us." So, when there are police officers who have a problem, we help them cover it up instead of help them recover from it. The system supports that approach.

So, what happens with a progressive disease such as alcoholism? It gets worse instead of better! If denial characterizes the disease of alcoholism, which we know it does, and if you don't say anything to me about my drinking, then you are reinforcing my denial. You've just become part of my problem. That's by and large what law enforcement does to its members who have problems, and I had a problem.

I'll give you an example. One police chief was quoted as saying, "I don't have any alcoholics because I have a rule against it." I understood that to mean, "Police officers can't have problems." Therefore, if I was to be a good police chief, I certainly couldn't have any problems. So my perception was

47

that if I could hide my drinking rather than deal with it, I would be OK. If, on the other hand, I reached out for help, I would be condemned. Even if my problem wasn't known publicly, I would still be making an admission that I had a weakness, and that was not acceptable in the profession.

Now, how do we reinforce that attitude? In 1976, when my doctor had told me that I was suffering from stress rather than alcoholism, he said I was too young at age thirty to be an alcoholic. Shortly after that, I took a course in stress management for police officers. Eight of us went out for lunch to discuss the class. A captain from another department said, "I don't know why we are listening to this garbage. If you got a police officer with a problem, you get rid of him." Now, I knew I had a problem, but I wasn't going to tell *this* guy about it. So I said, "Wait a minute. If you had two police officers, and they had identical problems, and one officer went and got help and the other one didn't, would you treat them the same or differently?" He said, "Differently, of course." I said, "How?" He said, "I'd fire the officer that gets help. The other guy can handle his own problems." So I took that information, coupled with what I heard the other police chief saying—"We don't have any alcoholics because we have a rule against it"— and I went back to drinking for another ten months, trying to figure out how to resolve my problems without doing anything about it! That's how the law enforcement system tends to reinforce people's staying sick.

A good share of the job that I do now, at Milwaukee Psychiatric Hospital, is convincing people that if they don't get help they are going to lose their careers and if they do get help they're not. Most can understand that if they don't get help they are going to lose their careers, but they also think that if they *do* get help the situation is not going to be any better. It is no more acceptable to be a recovering alcoholic than it is to be an active one.

•

So, what happened to me? Over a period of time, I wound up addicted to prescribed medication as well as alcohol. I didn't get into trouble at work, for a couple of reasons. I suspect one of them was because I was the chief. People didn't challenge me. Another reason is that when you take Valium, you don't have to drink during the day. Just to show you how perverted my logic became, when the doctor told me that I shouldn't drink when I'm taking Valium and to take Valium three times a day, I took it at seven, ten, and two, and didn't start drinking until four-thirty! That made perfect sense to me. So I didn't have to drink when I was working. I took my pills when I was working. You can't smell Valium.

I was an absolute jerk as a chief during this period of time—very short-tempered, arbitrary, kind of heavy-handed. But I didn't get into any trouble at work because of my addictions.

In 1976, however, an allegation was made that I had accepted a bribe. I had not even been offered the bribe, so the allegation was false, but I couldn't handle the allegation and I dove even deeper into the bottle in an attempt to escape from the pain of trying to figure the situation out. Everybody else is innocent until proven guilty, but police officers are guilty until they are proven innocent. How do you prove you didn't accept a cash bribe?

As a result, I wound up in the hospital, in the psych unit. Even then, I didn't understand that my primary problem was my drinking. I thought it was my reaction to the bribery investigation. When I came out of the hospital, instead of coming out knowing that I was an alcoholic and trying to recover, I came out with even more medication. The psychiatrist thought my depression was worsened by the Valium, which is a central nervous system depressant, so he put me on Valium *and* an antidepressant *and* sleeping pills. I was also drinking about three quarts of brandy a week at home.

I went on like this for another year until I got so sick that in 1977 I went into treatment and finally got some help for my alcoholism. Today, it has been over thirteen years since my last drink and my last pill. When I entered treatment I had been the chief of police at State Fair Park for three years. I was thirty-three years old. I had an associate degree in police science. And I was *not* active in the Episcopal church.

•

At about the same time I went into treatment, my wife and I decided it would be a good idea to go back to church. Our kids were growing up and we felt they needed to be raised in the church. I think it said more about our own needs, but we weren't able to verbalize that at the time. The superficial reason for going back to the church was for our children.

We transferred from the downtown parish where Peg had been assaulted to St. Edmund's in the suburb of Elm Grove. I was coming out of treatment at the time, and the rector there was very supportive of my recovery. He learned that we had been very active in the church before and immediately got us active in St. Edmund's. I owe him a deep debt of gratitude. He accepted me in a way that I had not anticipated being accepted. I suppose such treatment ought to be the norm, but I didn't expect it.

Meanwhile, Peg and I were becoming active in AA and Al-Anon. I discovered a new sense of spirituality there. I had been an agnostic for some years. I always believed that the world was more than an accident, but I certainly had gotten to the point where I didn't think there was a God who was personally responsive to Tom Winslow.

I became very active in AA. Over a period of time I realized that there were too many things that had happened in my life to label them coincidence: the fact that I had not gotten into significant trouble on the job; the fact that people had been placed in my life at the right time. As much as I say that that captain who sat across the table from me at the stress management seminar was part of what helped me deny my alcoholism, twelve or thirteen years later I'm still telling the story, so he must have had some impact on me, even if it was in retrospect. I don't regret the past or wish to close the door on it. It's all part of my understanding of where I came from and how I got to where I am today.

•

A lot of wonderful things began to happen. In about 1980, two years into my own recovery, I was asked to teach a class on alcoholism within law enforcement. When I was first asked, I was aghast. "How can I do this?" I decided there were two things I had to do if I was going to teach the class. First, I had to be willing to say I was a recovering alcoholic, because this was a class that involved teaching groups of twenty-five to thirty police officers on a weekly basis, a different group every week, in an in-service routine. It went on for eighteen to twenty sessions, so it included 500 to 600 police officers. I knew somebody was going to ask if I was an alcoholic, and I had to be willing to tell each class the same thing.

I went to a friend of mine who was a physician and who treated impaired physicians. I said, "I don't think I want to become a role model for police officers." He said, "Do you think what I'm doing with doctors is wrong?" I said No. He said, "Get out there and start teaching!" He explained to me that if all of us who are recovering alcoholics stayed in the closet, the only alcoholic police officers anybody would see would be the ones who were still sick. Those of us who were getting well wouldn't be identified as alcoholics. He said somebody had to be willing to risk, to talk about the fact that you can get well and still stay in your profession.

The day I went into treatment I was utterly convinced that making the decision to enter treatment meant that I was giving up my job and my career in law enforcement. Now, it didn't happen that way, but that was how far I had to go. I don't want other police officers to have to do that. There has to be a way to let police officers know that if you develop a problem you can get help, and you're not going to lose your job because you get help.

So I said OK, but there was one more thing I had to do. I was one of twenty-three police chiefs in Milwaukee County. If I was going to teach this course, I was going to have to do a presentation for the Milwaukee Metropolitan Police Chiefs Association. Prior to my doing that presentation there were only three police chiefs in Milwaukee County that knew I was a recovering alcoholic. Everybody that was at the meeting knew about it afterwards. That was October of 1980, and in November of 1980 they elected me their president. That began a process of validation of myself and my approach to alcoholism among police officers that was totally unexpected by me.

I began teaching classes for police officers on alcoholism in law enforcement. Part of what happened as a result was that I became a resource for other police chiefs. If the police chief in a suburb had a problem with an officer, he would call me and say, "Hey, Tom, I've got this guy with a problem. Would you come down and talk to him?" I'd go down and talk to him, and he'd give me his line of bull and I'd cut through it because I'd already been there. I'd help him get into treatment and help him get back to work. Of course, we also had a little leverage with these cops, because by the time they called me it was already at the point where they either accept the help that Chief Winslow was offering them or face the disciplinary approach. It was like, "You can do this the easy way or the hard way, take your pick."

•

At the same time, one of our priests in the Episcopal church was recovering. At the diocesan convention he proposed that a commission on alcoholism be created. It was a two-day session, and I spent the whole first night wondering if I should get up the next morning and second this resolution. Once again, I knew that if I was going to do that I would have to say that

I was recovering myself. They needed to know what my bias was if I was going to say something favorable. I had a very difficult time trying to determine if I needed to say something because it needed to be said, or because Tom Winslow wanted to be the big shot again, standing up in front of a crowd. I prayed a lot about it that night and decided that somebody needed to stand up and support this resolution. The church at the time thought that all the alcoholics were out on skid row. There were a lot of us who were recovering that were in the mainstream of the church. Once again, it was the whole business about unless you testify about your addiction—at least below the level of press, radio, and films, which is the AA philosophy of self-disclosure—how's anyone going to know there are recovering people in their midst?

The next day I seconded the resolution. The bishop's response was, "Well, now we have our first two volunteers." I've been serving on the Commission on Alcoholism ever since. When we started meeting, my wife sent a letter to the bishop saying, "You have all these recovering alcoholics on the commission, why aren't families involved?" He sent a letter back to her saying, "Thank you for volunteering," and Peg is a past chair of the Commission on Alcoholism.

We began by doing parish presentations. These were just some fairly simple parish education programs on alcoholism as a disease from which people can get well. We found out that some of the worst enablers of alcoholics out there were clergy who were giving inappropriate sympathy, so they were helping people stay sick instead of helping them get well. We put together a workshop and started training clergy in intervention techniques.

The result was the same as with starting to train police officers. Peg and I started getting calls at home saying, "I've got a parishioner who's got a real problem and I don't know what to do. Can you help?" We then became resources in the Episcopal church for clergy throughout southern Wisconsin trying to get help for people who had problems with alcohol and drugs.

•

The commission grew, and so did our ministry in that area. In 1980, about the same time I started teaching law enforcement, I participated in the ordination of a friend to the diaconate. At the rehearsal I was surprised to hear the part of the examination of the candidate which says, "You are to make Christ and his redemptive love known by your word and example to those among whom you live and work and worship. You are to interpret to the church the needs, concerns and hopes of the world." I suddenly realized that what the church says about deacons was what we were doing in the Commission on Alcoholism. Once again I was faced with the call to ordained ministry.

I had been raised with the idea that I ought to become an Episcopal priest. I had a great aunt, for example, who said she wasn't going to die until I could bury her. I'm still not a priest, and she died fifteen years ago! I think the reasons I didn't pursue the priesthood were my own feelings of inadequacy. The analogy I use is that throughout my life I kept putting this vocation on the shelf, and the thing kept falling off the shelf and hitting me on the head. Well, you know something can only hit you on the head so many times before you say, "Something must be going on here."

I went to my rector and soon began the process towards ordination. In 1983 I was ordained a deacon in the Episcopal church and given a nonparochial assignment as a staff person on the Commission on Alcoholism.

•

I have became acutely aware that if people were going to get help in recovery from chemical dependency, one of the aspects that has the most impact on them is their jobs. In the beginning, I thought it made a difference whether it was law enforcement or nursing, for example. In the long run what I found out is that the type of work doesn't make any difference, but everyone thinks it does.

I've learned that if you've got a police officer who is alcoholic, for example, and you want to get him or her some help, the people who can help the most are other police officers. If you have a nun who has an alcohol problem, the people who can help the most are other nuns. If you have a physician who has a problem, the people who have the most impact are other physicians. And so I began to do things which would involve peers in helping people accept help for their problems.

In 1985 the doctors that I now work for came to me and said, "Would you come and help us work with people in different professions?" I said No. I had graduated from the FBI Academy in 1984 and promised the FBI I would stay in law enforcement for three years. I still had two years to go on that obligation. So I said, "I'm not going anywhere," and I didn't.

In 1987, when my obligation to the FBI had expired, however, the doctors came back and made me an offer I couldn't refuse. I became the coordinator of the Professional Program at Milwaukee Psychiatric Hospital. I am now paid to do what I used to do as a volunteer. A great deal of my time is spent, not just with police officers, but with a whole host of people in different jobs for whom I try to develop peer support. Peer support is important in helping people recover. I continue to do that in law enforcement and in the church. I do interventions with clergy, doctors, and lawyers. I serve as liaison between the treatment team and some vocationally focused self-help groups, such as International Doctors in AA; Lawyers Concerned for Lawyers; The Recovered Alcoholic Clergy Association; Law Enforcement Officers Concerned; and the Wisconsin Impaired Pharmacist Program.

•

My whole life has come together. When I say I am a deacon, people say, "What parish are you in?" I say, "Well, if you

55

really want to understand the diaconate, you have to understand servant ministry. What I'm doing every day of my life is diaconal in nature. I happen to be the assistant at St. David's in New Berlin, but that's only where I go on Sunday mornings."

In the church we have a parochial mind-set. They say, "What do you *do*?" And you tell them and they say, "Yes, but what *parish* are you in?" Does it make any difference? Actually, my parish is part of my support system. Most of my ministry is not parochial in nature. What I do full-time at the hospital, or with the Commission on Alcoholism for the diocese, is my ministry.

Step 11 of AA says, "Seek through prayer and meditation to improve our conscious contact with God as we understand him, praying only for knowledge of his will for us and the power to carry that out." What I finally figured out is that there is a wholeness to my life and a sense of mission. The hospital, the church, and AA are what provide the context within which I fulfill my ministry.

Comments by the Authors

Attitudes are changing since the days when that captain said, "I'd fire the officer that gets help." Today more and more law enforcement agencies are recognizing that it is in their own best interest to have substance-abuse rehabilitation programs in place and confidentially available. It is also in the best interest of individual officers. Besides the support of the department, officers also need the support of their fellow workers when they seek substance-abuse counseling. Squad partners and other co-workers do no one a favor when they cover up a fellow officer's substance-abuse problems.

The twelve steps followed by Alcoholics Anonymous groups show how closely related a healthy spirituality and an alcohol-free life-style can be. This healthy spirituality is reflected in the ability to do a good day's work and to relate to one's fellow workers without being an "absolute jerk."

Winslow discovered the importance of small-group dynamics among groups of peers. He discovered that honesty with himself and with others had a rehabilitative effect. He successfully pulled himself out of a destructive alcoholic situation and moved into a position where he could and did help others. He did so in connection with Alcoholics Anonymous after his alcoholism had reached crisis levels. However, there is no reason why support groups could not be developed for officers to attend before major problems arise with their health or job performance. Such groups might be instrumental in preventing abuse of alcohol, drugs, or other addictive or destructive behaviors.

Winslow has pointed to the importance of having departmental support when seeking help for problems that impair job performance. Departments need to have policies in place before the need arises for individual officers. The problems are there for all to see, if administrators are honest with themselves. The solutions can also be found among the literature and training departments of major law enforcement agencies. It may take a little research, but solutions are available.

Being "enamored of this new life in law enforcement" draws many officers away from a spiritually healthy life. This may happen not only because of fascination with the work itself, but also because any diversion of an officer's attention may be thought of as being in competition with full commitment to the "brotherhood in blue." Maintaining a life apart from the department is especially hard for rookies, who have the most difficult schedules and who are the most eager to fit into the stereotypical life-style and image of law enforcement officers.

In addition, the need for secrecy and security encourages officers to give up outside involvements and to interact primarily with other officers who have similar interests and responsibilities. It is a "them-against-us" mentality. The healthier a person's spirit is, the more likely it is that the person will be drawn into community activities that include people with many interests and occupations. The fact that people argue themselves into the position that avoids contact with the community might be a good reason for them to look deeper into their own spirituality and to ask how healthy it really is. Winslow points to an attitude that could profitably be nurtured by people everywhere. God is in the world, and it is *in the world* that the ministry of God's people needs to take place.

•4•

JOSÉ REYES

I'm Going to Change That

Speaking the language of the people

Police Officer José Reyes came to the United States from Puerto Rico in 1970. He dreamed of becoming a police officer and thought he could help people who did not speak English by translating for them. He likes police work and enjoys helping people. He works in the Juvenile Division, Milwaukee Police Department. He says God and the church have been important in helping him deal with the tensions of police work. He also finds support within his family. Officer José Reyes is Lutheran.

I came to Milwaukee in March of 1970. I was always interested in becoming a police officer, ever since I was ten or eleven years old. My uncle was a police department captain in Puerto Rico, where people had a lot of respect for the police.

I came to the United States to get ahead. I was raised on a farm in Puerto Rico. There were thirteen children in our family. No electricity. No running water. We had cows, horses, and chickens, but not a lot of money.

My uncle gave me the money to come to the States. When I came here, I went out the next day and found a job in a factory. I have been working ever since.

•

My uncle, the captain in the police department, went through the ranks real fast—an intelligent guy. He had a nervous breakdown partly because of the stress of police work. What triggered the breakdown was a religious retreat. His wife was a religious person—a real devout Catholic. My uncle wasn't that religious. He said religion turned him off. His wife finally convinced him to go on one of those weekend retreats for couples. He came out of there and apparently just snapped. He was placed on disability for a while but he is now back in the department doing limited duty work. He is near retirement. Today he is one of the most religious persons I know. I don't think you'd call him a fanatic, but I've seen him talking to people, trying to convert people or to help them realize there is a God who can change things for them—who can give them a better life.

I used to be Catholic, too, but I met the woman who would be my wife and six months later we were married. She was Lutheran, of German descent. Her Lutheran congregation was real good to me. They treated me with respect. I think I was the only Hispanic in that congregation. Now, I am on the Board of Elders. We have two meetings a month to discuss church affairs. We also make calls on people from the congregation.

•

I met my wife before I became a police officer. When I told her I was thinking of applying for the police department, she said, "If that is what you want to do, go ahead." She supported me all along, helping out. She still does. When I call my home and tell her what time I will be home or whatever, she asks, "You're all right, aren't you?" She is concerned about my safety, but she doesn't want me to leave police work.

My sister got robbed one time when we first came to the United States. We went to the police station; she didn't speak any English and there was no one to translate for us. I was still pretty young and my English wasn't very good. It was hard for us to communicate with the police. So, I said, "Someday, I'm going to change that."

It took me five years to finally make it on the force. There was a height requirement in the department at that time. You had to be 5'8" to apply for police officer, so I went to school for a while. As soon as the height restriction was lifted, I took the police exam but I failed it. I said, "I'm going to try it again," and enrolled in Milwaukee Area Technical College. I took the police exam again in 1975 and this time I passed. I was one of the first Hispanics to enter the Milwaukee Police Department.

•

The vice squad took me when I first came in. They used me right away. I was working undercover for three months or so. It was an essential operation. Then I went back in uniform. After two years I went back to the vice squad for about two years. Those years were bad for me because of the stress and tension. You really have to deal with hard criminal elements in the vice squad. People are dealing drugs. You have to go into taverns and meet those people, and I was drinking too much at that time.

When you are in the vice squad, the department gives you money to spend on drinks. You stand out if you don't drink. If you drink juice or Coke in a bar, people look at you funny; you become a suspicious character.

One time I got home from work and my wife said, "Either you quit drinking or you get the door." I said, "I'll quit drinking." I did it on my own. No groups. I just quit. I was not in the narcotics division at that time, so drinking on the job wasn't required.

When I worked undercover, I dealt with gambling. As a result, I was threatened by some of the gamblers. They put a contract out on me. The department put two officers outside of my home at all times, twenty-four hours a day. Wherever I or my family went, we had to call for a squad to take us there. They gave me a bulletproof vest. After a while, the constant presence of bodyguards gets to be a pain. The department was good about it, though. They didn't hesitate to put a "plant" outside our house, and the guys were real good. After a few years I finally felt safe and requested that they send no more plants.

The gamblers were still upset about me, however. You cannot befriend people and then suddenly arrest them, and I arrested the whole bunch of them, I guess twenty-five or so, up to the top of the operation. We were supposed to be "brothers," so they felt betrayed by me. But I had done nothing wrong. They had.

•

I have done so many things in the police department. It is hard to describe any one event as standing out from the rest. Each incident is different, no two are the same. All police work is good work, and it can be fascinating. No matter what kind of investigation you do, whether it is child abuse or whatever the case may be, it's interesting and good to be helpful.

There is one incident, though, that is impossible for me to forget. A person died as a result of it. It happened in 1986, about three o'clock in the afternoon. We just happened to be driving by and a lady said, "Hey, those people there just robbed a woman." I saw the car pulling away. I followed it and got to the intersection. When I got there I said to my partner, "Put the emergency lights on." Instead of him putting the lights on, however, he picked up the radio and broadcast a description of the car. I was paying attention to driving the car and didn't notice that he hadn't turned the lights on.

Suddenly my partner yelled, "Look out!" Another car was driving northbound on Ninth street. I hit the car. Bang! There was a guy coming southbound on a Moped, a scooter. The car I hit ran into him and killed him. I thought he was dead (or at least in very critical condition) when I picked him up. We called an ambulance and went to the hospital. They treated everyone's injuries. I suffered a back injury that still hurts sometimes. When I got home, the first thing I did was to call my pastor and tell him what happened. He came over to my house and we prayed for the guy who was hit to survive. I told my pastor I didn't mean to cause an accident. It was just part of the danger related to the job, but I still feel bad about it. The man did eventually die.

There was a departmental investigation that left me kind of bitter. After the pastor came to my house, and while I had relatives in the house, the sergeant came and wanted to know what happened. He wanted me to give a statement. I refused because I didn't know if it was going to be a fatal accident. I had been advised not to make any statements. So he said, "Listen, I am going to issue you a citation for failure to yield the right of way." I had a stop sign, and the car I hit did not. Based on that, I guess, they decided to issue the citation against me.

What bothered me is that they came to my house and issued the citation and took my driver's license away. The citation eventually was dismissed in court. The District Attorney said it was just an accident, that there was no intent to cause the death of this person. But it bothered me for quite a while.

Then lawyers came to my house and said they were putting a lien on my house. They put two, three liens against my house. The family of the victim sued. The hospital sued the police department because they said I was in the wrong and the person I hit didn't have any insurance. The lady that I hit also filed suit against the city. It took quite a while to get everything back to normal.

Faith in God helped. Every Sunday the pastor said he would pray for me, and the congregation was pulling for me. It's funny how one incident can change your life. For example, I was really upset about this incident, but my wife has a strong faith. She kept saying, "We'll make it, don't worry about it." She had enough strength for both of us to cope with the situation. I still remember the date of that incident, that's how much it affected me. My wife knows it too. She will say, "Oh, I know what is bothering you today." When that date comes around each year, the incident is again fresh in my mind.

•

Under a previous administration, the chief chose his own people for promotions. I was a good undercover police officer. I risked my life and everything else. There were five of us working together. One made sergeant. Three made detective. I am the only one who didn't get promoted. I passed the exam like the others. The others were all white. I was the only Hispanic. There was discrimination against some good white police officers, too. They just didn't belong to the same "in" group, politically. That's why the police department was so screwed up back then. They didn't promote people for their abilities or background. They promoted people for their political connections. There were excellent officers who passed the exams, but because they weren't close to the chief or to a captain, they weren't promoted.

We couldn't speak openly about it back then because some of the guys we worked with would report it back to our superiors. You had to be careful what you would say. I didn't expect that when I became an officer. I expected I would be working with grown-up people—responsible people. I got upset about it sometimes. I asked myself, "Why am I doing this work?" If I would have filed a grievance, I would have been given the lousiest assignment in the world, walking the beat in the worst possible neighborhood.

I haven't taken the last three or four promotional exams. I am working days now. If you are promoted, you have to go back working nights again. It's not worth it. I am going to take one more promotional exam, but not until I get closer to retirement.

My wife wants me to take the promotional exam again. The last couple of times she said, "You should take it, you should take it." I joked with her, "What, do you want to spend nights by yourself or something?"

The kids do better when I am home nights. About a month after I started working days I could see the difference with the children. The kids would do their homework. Before that, they didn't care so much. Their grades improved. I could see the change right away. It was worth it to be home with them. It doesn't make any sense for you to have a lot of money from a promotion if your kids are all mixed up. There is no money value on that. We will survive financially, even though we're not that well off.

•

When police deal with Hispanic citizens, there are some things they should keep in mind. Hispanics like to be treated with respect. The older generation, when they talk to you, will tell you the truth. A lot of times police officers tend not to believe what civilians say. If an officer calls a Hispanic person a liar, the person loses respect for the officer. That person is not going to give the officer any more information or help solve a crime. So the problem is with the police officers. If an officer lies to them and says, for example, "I am going to do this or that for you," and then he doesn't come through, then a Hispanic will say "I don't like him. He's a liar."

Hispanics respect police in general. When I first came into the department, many Hispanic people in Milwaukee didn't know English. And the officers didn't know any Spanish. When there was any communication problem between the police and a citizen, they would bring someone in to translate. But translators miss the more subtle communications that take place. For example, when I ask you a question, the way that I ask you the question determines the answer I get. Then, by the response that I get, I know more or less whether you are sincere. But, if we don't know each other's language and get someone to translate, all that person does is translate words, not emotions.

For example, you can look a person in the eye and say, "Hey, I feel sorry for you," and mean it. But if a translator says, "He feels sorry for you," it doesn't carry the same message. The real feeling has been lost in the translation. Translators should not be given formulated questions by cops to translate word for word. They should form the police officer's questions themselves in the style of the language they are speaking and according to that culture.

When I go out to translate for some detectives, I say, "Tell me what's going on. Tell me what happened and what you want to know." Then I will ask the citizens the questions. I ask the questions myself in Spanish, rather than letting the detective formulate the questions and then translating. That way the person gets the questions firsthand.

The problem we are having today is that the police officers who do speak Spanish don't know how to write it or read it. They grew up hearing their relatives speak Spanish, but they went to schools where they had to read and write in English. Bilingual schools would definitely be an advantage. My kids know how to read, write, and speak Spanish—not perfectly, but they can get along.

In many cases the police take a confession, but don't know how to write or read Spanish. One case went to court and they brought in a professional who asked, "How do you know if this confession didn't violate his constitutional rights when you don't even know how to write or read Spanish?" So the confession was thrown out.

Another problem we have with the lack of police officers who speak Spanish is the difficulty Hispanics have in getting into the department. In addition to the written exam, recruits have to pass a background investigation that includes talking with the recruit's neighbors. Many times the neighbors of Hispanic applicants do not speak English, yet the department sends out investigators who do not speak Spanish. This makes it hard for recruits to pass the background investigation. The department should send out trained officers who are fluent in Spanish. This would put the neighbors at ease and allow them to talk in their own language.

Police officers have been held in high regard by Hispanics, but I believe that police work has been perceived by them as a male profession and not a female profession. In fact, women make very good police officers. Hispanics think that in this profession you are always fighting with people. That is not really the case. Police life is mostly helping people out rather than fighting or shooting people. We have about 1,800 officers in our department and only a few are ever involved in a shooting. Of course, if I got into a situation where I had to use a gun I wouldn't hesitate to do it, but it's not a thing that happens all the time, the way they show on television.

•

I myself don't think about fighting or shooting. I start the day by asking myself "How can I help somebody today?" It gives me satisfaction that I can help people in my work. For example, a woman called yesterday. Her daughter is sixteen and ran away from home. She wanted to talk to someone who would listen to her. So that's what I did. I spent about a half hour with her. I listen to people who have had crimes committed against them, too. These are good people. When you hear their stories you want to find the person who did a bad thing to them. This is the satisfaction police officers get, helping the good people.

67

On the other hand, police officers like to see the crooks punished. The problem today is that people are not being punished for the wrongs they do. The court system, judges, and district attorneys don't seem to be that effective. When offenders do get convicted they don't seem to get the punishment their crimes deserve. I am now dealing with juveniles and I see that the kids are out of jail the next day after they are arrested. The courts let these young hoodlums back out on the streets. It's sad.

Sure the jails are crowded. Right now the Milwaukee County Juvenile Detention Center can only hold 108 people, but 120 kids are sent there, so they have to release twelve. It's mandatory. They have to decide who, of all the kids, is the least likely to do more harm out there!

From day one they should let kids know the rules. If they commit an offense, especially armed burglaries, robberies, and such, these kids should be put in a place where they don't get so many privileges—a place where they have to work, maybe dig holes eight hours a day for a week. They'll think twice about it before they commit another offense.

That's the way it used to be back home. When I was a kid in Puerto Rico, if a kid committed a crime, they arrested him or her, and they arrested either the father or the mother. The parents were responsible for their child's actions until he or she was eighteen years old. The parents had to pay whatever restitution had to be made. The kid was put in detention. Usually the parents were charged and put on probation. Here in the United States, the parents are not charged and the kid has to be waived to adult court in order to be charged with a serious crime.

If parents are responsible for the child until he or she is eighteen, then parents should be held responsible if there is a crime committed. Maybe a kid goes out and does not come home until late at night, and the parents don't say anything. Maybe they see something on TV about an incident and don't ask the kid any questions. When I was a boy and came home with money or a new toy or something, my parents always asked, "Where did you find that? Who gave it to you?" If I didn't have answers, I was in trouble.

The same thing with school. The parents back home would tell the teacher, "If he doesn't behave, just let us know." The education system in the States is different. Here, the kid comes home and tell the parents "The teacher yelled at me," and the parents file a law suit against the teacher! They can only do so much without the parents' cooperation and discipline.

Parents have to start with discipline when the kid is one or two years old. If you wait until the kid is thirteen or fourteen, it is not going to work. My children are real good. They are not into drinking or smoking. They get good grades. It might be old fashioned, but it works.

•

Somehow, God pushes us to do the best we can do as police officers. I feel we are acting on behalf of God in our work. Very few people who become police officers say it is because of the money. They become officers because they want to help other people in the community. What happens, however, is they become disgusted with the system—the way things are done. One way to deal with these feelings is to go home and pray for the people who are doing things you don't like. If he is your sergeant, and he treats you badly, pray for him. Some-day, somehow, something will happen to change things.

Comments by the Authors

The story shared with us by Officer Reyes reveals a person with a very positive outlook in spite of the difficulties he has encountered, both internally and externally. Height restric-tions, a difficult entrance exam, promotional practices that left him out, threats against his life, the dangers of stress and alcohol, could all have taken their toll and discouraged a less determined person. Reyes patiently dealt with each obstacle as it arose, finding a solution to each problem.

Officer Reyes was willing to go for more schooling when he failed the entrance exam. He was willing to listen to the advice of his wife, who probably knows him better than anyone else. And he was astute enough to keep his priorities straight by putting the welfare of his children and their success ahead of a promotion that might jeopardize their grades in school. The results reveal a satisfying and successful career and a solid family life.

Officer Reyes helps us understand the situation of both the citizens and the police when they can't communicate with each other. That can lead to failure to cooperate with each other and also to difficulties getting Hispanic officers into the police department. Failure to pass the background investigation or growing distrust between Hispanics and the police can be caused simply by an inability to communicate. Sometimes when we are in school facing a second language requirement we may think of it as just a waste of time. However, Reyes points out the need for officers who cannot only speak the language of the people but can also read and write the language. This would be true not only of Spanish but also of other languages prevalent in our society.

Any law enforcement department should reflect the make-up of the community it serves, not only part of it. It is disappointing to hear that police departments may have, in the past, had policies and practices that kept some capable people out of leadership positions or even out of the department. Height restrictions, age restrictions, and such can be deterrents to developing a healthy law enforcement agency and can be discouraging to potential applicants who think they don't stand a chance to be admitted or promoted. Patience helps, but so does an honest challenge to restrictions that might be unnecessary barriers to good law enforcement. Departments need to regularly assess their personnel practices.

Officer Reyes has maintained an active role in his church, even though he changed his denomination because of his marriage. It is not always easy for an officer to schedule time for church activities, but José Reyes shows how it has helped him spiritually to be involved in a faith community *before* a time of crisis. Both his pastor and his fellow parishioners stood at his side with prayers and support when he faced the trauma of being injured himself and being involved in another person's death. One can never predict when such a tragic event will happen. When it does, it helps to have already established a relationship with God and a faith community.

• 5 •

NATALIE AIKINS

I'm Going to Keep Coming Back

Domestic violence and child abuse

Natalie Aikins is an officer with the Madison Police Department, Madison, Wisconsin. She tells us about sex discrimination on the job, as well as her experience with domestic violence victims, runaway children, and alcohol abusers. Aikins has taken what she learned on her police job into the church to develop programs on these topics. She is a member of the Episcopalian church.

There is no way to start this story without telling about when I first decided I wanted to be a police officer. My mother is a fundamentalist Christian. My father is a Methodist. When I went home at thirty-one years old (in 1977), married with two kids and a house in the suburbs, and told my folks that I was trying for the police department, my mom promptly said that she was going to pray that I didn't get the job. She didn't believe that women should be doing this work. Not only did she believe women should not be doing this kind of work, but she worried that I'd be taking a job away from a man. She would also be concerned about my safety. So she was going to pray that I wouldn't be hired.

Given my upbringing, I was sure I wasn't going to get the job, because I knew God listened to my mom's prayers! When I did get the job, it was a really strange feeling that maybe sometimes what Mom prayed for wasn't necessarily God's will. I believed that if it was God's will that I got the job, then I'd get it. That's what *I* prayed for.

So the story really starts there. When I got married, I was received into the Episcopalian church because that's what my husband Bob's religion was. He had been a cradle Episcopalian. I had an eclectic background before that. As a child, I had a good grounding in Bible teaching from Mom. I went to the Methodist church as a kid. When I got out on my own, I left town and went to Washington to live with an aunt and uncle. They were involved in the Lutheran church, so I went with them. So, my background was varied.

At the time I got the job with the police department, I didn't think about it much in relation to my religion, other than that I had a strong belief that people would be treated differently because of who I was and because of my faith. I thought that if I had anything to bring to policing, it was who I am not only as a female, but as a Christian. Other than that, I really didn't think much about how my faith would affect or impact my career.

That was at a time when we were integrating the police force in terms of gender. I never thought much about being in an icebreaker situation, because there had been women in the Madison Police Department since 1974. This was three years later. It never occurred to me that we were still—and for a long time—going to be working at that. It never crossed my mind that discrimination was going to be a problem, but it was. Madison now has 80 sworn female officers, which is 25% of our total sworn personnel.

There were some times on the job when, in retrospect, I realize the only thing that kept me going was God. There were times when I was ready to just pull the plug and say, "This is not for me. I can't handle any more of this."

The main problems were internal. I didn't have any trouble with the public. Well, I shouldn't say I didn't have *any* trouble. I didn't have any trouble handling any perception the public might have had about women in police work. That was just not nearly as much of a problem as trying to integrate the work force internally. That was the most difficult part of those early years.

I remember one situation in which I was checking an accident. A fellow officer from another department was at fault in the accident, according to witnesses. I just didn't have any choice but to deal with it as I would any other situation. The off-duty officer was cited as at fault in the accident.

It wasn't twenty minutes later, at the garage when I was gassing up, that one of my colleagues came in my face about who did I think I was to be treating a fellow officer like that and making those kinds of decisions. *That* was a real scary situation! I hadn't treated the officer at fault any differently than I would have treated anyone else. If I had felt that I could have given anyone else a break, I would have given my fellow cop a break, but there was just no choice. There were witnesses, and it was like anything else where you just do what you have to do. You do your job.

That was my first run-in with the expectation that you do your job differently when other officers are involved. At least some people have those expectations. I really had trouble after that incident when I was working the night shift, because I just didn't get backup sometimes, for things that were normally "hot calls" where everybody should be screeching in. And that was scary. But it also taught me a good lesson about my own resources and God being there to take care of us. This is in retrospect, however. At the time, I don't remember thinking much about it. But, in trying to put all of this stuff that I've learned on the job into perspective, everything that I have done in my career in law enforcement has prepared me for other ministries. It's hard when you are going through it to be able to see it as clearly. The first preparation was learning to trust myself and to trust God to take care of me.

•

After I had been in patrol for six years, I started looking for other things to do in the police force. I applied for, and got, a day job in safety education. I had been ready to quit the police force. I was the odd one out in my family. I was missing a lot of stuff with the kids at school, and even though Bob's hours were so flexible that the kids always had one of us there, I was the one person missing out. So I was ready to quit because I wasn't willing to sacrifice all of the things that were important to me in my family for my career. The job just wasn't important enough. I needed to find day work, which I finally found within the police department.

When I got the position in safety education, my focus was to create a program to teach children about child-abuse prevention. At that time the Madison Police Department had the Stranger Danger program. I had done enough research by that point to know that strangers weren't the problem. Children were being abused by people they knew. Yes, we do have enticement attempts, and children need to know how to deal with that, but we shouldn't create a whole generation of paranoid kids by teaching them not to talk to strangers.

I had my idea about what a child-abuse prevention program should look like, and during the next several years we got it going in the Madison schools. In fact, we got legislation passed to make it mandatory for all schools in the state to teach protective behaviors.

Another major focus for me was the whole issue of missing children. In law enforcement, we are learning that most of them are missing because they are running away from some sort of problem, or many such cases are custodial/parental kinds of abductions.

A couple of things I wish officers would keep in mind, especially when they are dealing with runaway children, is that most of them are running away from some issue or situation that they haven't been able to deal with. Instead of seeing them as troublemakers, or bad kids, or worse, we should understand that they are most likely in need of help. Even though they also need to learn to accept the consequences of their behavior, they should be given help in dealing with their problems.

•

Part of my job in public safety education has been to talk with youngsters about drug and alcohol abuse. Teaching that information to kids prepared me to deal with—or at least gave me a better handle on—dealing with our family when my husband's brother died from complications of alcoholism.

That may not be a typical law enforcement story, but I feel it is. Because of the training that I received related to my job, I've had some measure of peace and understanding about the problems I've encountered in my own family life.

All that early learning has also led me further into ministry through the church. As a direct result of having a background in child abuse and domestic violence, and because of my work with the school district to develop a curriculum on substance abuse for children, I became active in the Alcoholism Commission of the Episcopal Diocese of Milwaukee and have been doing some training of clergy in the area of domestic violence and substance abuse.

I do volunteer work at Grace Church in Madison and with the diocesan team to train new parish teams in the catechumenal process we call Living Our Baptismal Covenant (LOBC). It is exciting, and I am involved because of my work. Which came first? I don't know. I think God has been preparing me for both all along.

•

Another example of this connection between the work of law enforcement and my religious experience is the area of death notifications, suicide, and families in crisis. I know, for instance, that my being a Christian female has made a difference in the way I handle domestic violence calls. Women and children have been so disenfranchised by the church in that area. I think of one domestic violence call specifically. I worked the east side a lot, at nights, and I had probably been to this same address eight or ten times over a couple of years. Every time I had gone, I would ask the woman if there wasn't somewhere that she and the kids could go for safety, but she always said no.

One night, the woman's ten-year-old son had called because his mommy was being beaten again. I got to the door and the ten-year-old let me in. His dad was standing not five feet behind him, ready to hit the boy. The dad told me I wasn't welcome there, but I said, "Well, your son let me in, and I need to check on the welfare of the rest of this family, because of the history here." This time was really no different than any other time I had been there, except this time the man got the message that I was going to keep coming back. He had seen me often enough to begin to realize that. It very often happens that the offender will be standing there saying, "You can't come in," but I will always check out the call rather than ignore it, regardless of how many times I have gone there or how many threats I have heard.

I remember that night asking the mother if there wasn't somebody who would take her in. Did she belong to a church? Was there someone in her parish who could help? She said that her pastor had already told her this was her lot in life. Finally, I got her to believe that she would be safe at the battered women's shelter, and that staying home and continuing to get beaten was not going to solve the problem or help her or the kids.

I think—partly because of the new domestic-abuse law—more and more law enforcement officers are willing to take on domestic violence calls. But when I first started this job, the majority of officers would ignore them. They would say, "It's a family affair. We shouldn't be involved."

•

Another example of ignoring a situation is child abuse, including incest. We still have cases in Madison where physicians are failing to report families where a child has been a victim of incest because they claim that's better dealt with in the medical community than by the law.

I think we have a better response in Madison on the part of the medical community than in a lot of other places. The fact is, however, that medical personnel don't have the understanding of the dynamics of abuse that law enforcement officers do. Doctors and nurses don't always understand that if there aren't some severe consequences for these perpetrators, there is probably not going to be sufficient motive for them to change. It's like any other kind of addictive behavior. It has to be unlearned, and they have to want to change. Sometimes, I suppose, child abusers are successfully cured without the threat of legal intervention being held over their heads, but in most cases you are not even going to get them into treatment without that threat.

•

We recently had a case of a church organist who was charged with child molesting. He was found guilty. The judge sentenced him to probation and counseling. I talked with several people whose boys had been victimized by the organist. In every case where it had come to the attention of the parents, they had taken it to the pastor and, without fail, every one of the parents had decided to deal with it pastorally instead of getting the legal system involved. Pedophiles, especially, aren't likely to change their behavior with pastoral counseling only.

In all my years on the job, in all the domestic violence cases I ever went to, I never had one woman tell me that she had a pastor or someone in her parish that she could turn to for help. That tells me very clearly that our congregations are not looking at domestic violence or making themselves aware of it enough to open themselves up to that ministry. It's not something that happens in "nice" churches. We want our world to be nice and clean, without problems, and so we feel that if we don't talk about them, then they don't exist. Not that any church would deliberately turn a victim away, but we don't encourage people to share those needs.

Parishioners have to know that their clergyperson is open to hearing their concerns and is trained to handle these kinds of situations. This needs to be said from the pulpit in various ways: partly in spreading the message through the homilies and sermons, and partly by letting people know that "We know these are issues that happen in everybody's lives, not just over there somewhere."

For police officers, it's a lot easier to deal with an abuse case—whether it's child abuse, physical abuse, sexual abuse, substance abuse—when we accept the fact that an offender is, underneath it all, most likely a hurt kid. It helps keep us objective and nonjudgmental. It helps to get a case nailed down when a cop is not acting out of anger because of what someone has done.

For me it was especially hard to stay objective, especially in child-abuse cases. However, once I educated myself about the whole cycle of violence and came to realize that most abusers have been abused themselves and that it is a learned behavior, it got easier for me to remain calm. It also made me less threatening to the offender when I acknowledged the root causes underneath the surface, while maintaining the bottom line that all people are responsible for their own behavior.

•

Another difficult issue for police officers to deal with is the death of a child. One such death that sticks out in my mind, the worst one, was that of a sixteen-year-old boy who had committed suicide. He got a gun from his uncle and shot himself, and I had to notify the family.

That was the hardest incident for me, partly because my own kids were about that age. This family was like every other family and like my family. Sometimes parents do their best and still things happen that they just can't control. I remember crying with that dad, while we waited for mom to come home from work, and calling the pastor. Afterwards I had to face my sergeant. He told me if I couldn't keep my emotions under control, I didn't belong in a police job. That was a very difficult thing to accept, because I had done my job. I had done what I needed to do there. It was difficult to feel censured by my supervisor for my caring response.

•

Most cops come into this job wanting to make a difference in people's lives. We are idealistic in a lot of ways. I think all of us are. When that idealism gets challenged, some people get cynical and some people quit.

Officers who get burned out and need counseling are the same officers who also would never in a million years ask for help. My department has a good employee assistance program. More and more people are making use of it as word spreads that it is available and it is confidential, and that people aren't going to be sanctioned for using it.

I think getting a chaplaincy program at work is probably going to be the next thing I will work toward. I haven't had time to pursue it yet, but I'm going to make some phone calls to some of the agencies that have chaplaincy programs and pursue initiating one here. A chaplaincy program is another resource for people who are having trouble related to their job. It takes a long time to establish credibility in police work, however. Officers need to be sure that a chaplain is trustworthy and can be counted on to be not only a true help to people but also to keep his or her mouth shut about it. Cops are nothing if not concerned about trustworthiness and confidentiality.

People still have the idea that police officers are supposed to be able to handle their own problems. We are supposed to help other people handle *their* problems, but it's not OK for *us* to have problems. There are still departments that say they don't have alcohol problems in their department, for example, because they get rid of them. Madison is way out in front in recognizing problems and in offering people services.

•

I know cops who have said they could never talk to their pastor. I remember when I was going through the worst of the problems on the night shift. I came home and shared my concerns with my husband, Bob. He said, "You must be exaggerating. It can't possibly be true that police officers would treat each other like that." Bob had a tendency to discount and to deny some of what was going on, which added to my own doubts. I thought, "Gee, am I exaggerating this, or am I paranoid, or what is going on here?"

At that time, I did not have a pastor I could go to for help. We were at another church in town then, and there was no way I would have taken my concerns to that priest. A lot of this has to do with how open the priest is and how the individual perceives that openness. Maybe that priest would have understood my problems, but he sure never let me think he would understand. He believed that there was a traditional role for women, and that those who stepped out of that role were on their own. So I could never have gone to him for advice or assistance.

There were several other female officers on the force, so we started a women's support group. That led to the formation of the Wisconsin Association of Women Police. I was the charter president of that association. At our first meeting, we had twenty county and city officers. We built it up to 125 people by the time I turned it over to the next president.

•

Sometimes I just want to say, "OK, God, which chain are you jerking today?" I love what I've been doing. It's probably the most important work I've ever done. Not only the paid work in the police department but also the work in terms of the ministry for the church, the commissions on the catechumenate and alcoholism.

Mine has been an interesting journey. I sure didn't see the connections between my work and my religion at first. Even though the basic faith was there, I never really thought of my work as ministry until the last few years, when it became very clear to me that that's exactly what I have been doing.

Comments by the Authors

One topic that Officer Aikins brings up involves both the professional aspects of law enforcement and the spiritual aspects of an officer's life. She says, "At the time I got the job with the police department, I didn't think about it much in relation to my religion." Many cops don't think of their job as a vocation. Police officers, however, can hardly *not* do their job in reference to their religion if their spirituality has been shaped by a religious orientation. True faith is so much a part of one's identity that it cannot be laid aside when a person goes to work, like changing from leisure clothes into a uniform.

Furthermore, the job of law enforcement itself institutionalizes the kinds of activity that God asks of those who want to live religious lives. The following are just a few religious concepts that are carried out by law enforcement agencies:

Justice:
"But let justice roll down like waters, and righteousness like an everflowing stream" (Amos 5:24).

Emergency care of crime victims:

" 'A man was going down from Jerusalem to Jericho, and fell into the hands of robbers, who stripped him, beat him, and went away, leaving him half dead. Now by chance a priest was going down that road; and when he saw him, he passed by on the other side. . . . But a Samaritan while traveling came near him; and when he saw him, he was moved with pity. He went to him and bandaged his wounds. . . . Then he . . . brought him to an inn. . . . Which of these three, do you think, was a neighbor to the man who fell into the hands of the robbers?' . . . Jesus said to him; 'Go and do likewise' " (Luke 10:30-37).

Breaking up civil disturbances:

"Blessed are the peacemakers, for they will be called children of God" (Matt. 5:9).

These are just a few of the many examples of official functions performed by law enforcement officers in our society. We are so used to thinking of the separation of church and state that we forget that the functions performed by state or local government law enforcement officers are functions that are held as ideals by religious people, who advocate doing them out of compassion and love for their fellow humans. The fact that law enforcement agencies, instead of the priests of the Old Testament or the Middle Ages, now enforce the law does not make it any less a holy function done for the good of society. The fact that officers get paid to help wounded victims and to promote justice does not make their actions any less holy than if they did them purely out of personal concern for the victims. Cops do help victims, and they do it professionally. Police officers, in the line of duty, illustrate the ideal of service to their fellow citizens, and they do so at great personal risk to their own lives. They embody the ultimate religious ideal: "No one has greater love than this, to lay down one's life for one's friends" (John 15:13).

Even parts of law enforcement work that do not seem, at face value, to be religious are handled better with a spiritual orientation behind them. The motivation for doing one's job makes a big difference. Sometimes that spiritual motivation is all that keeps an officer doing the "dirty" jobs that need to be done. And sometimes God alone supports the officer in dangerous situations. "Whatever your task, put yourselves into it, as done for the Lord and not for your masters, since you know that from the Lord you will receive the inheritance as your reward; you serve the Lord Christ" (Col. 3:23-24).

Officer Aikins is working hard at bridging the gap between her life in a law enforcement agency and her life in the church. She is doing this by bringing the knowledge she gained as a police officer into the church, to educate and help people in that environment. She points to a number of areas that church members and officials need to address: domestic violence, drug and alcohol abuse, clergy/church member communication. Because of her experience as an officer, Aikins is able to offer quality educational programs to church members and leaders on these topics.

Her point is well taken that unless members hear church leaders and clergy say they are open to discussing domestic abuse, alcohol-related problems, and other touchy topics (such as AIDS), the members will not talk to church leaders or clergy about them. The church needs to have programs in place that deal with these problems, not hide its head in the sand and pretend the problems do not exist.

Even aside from specific social problems, the question of clergy/church member communication is a serious one. It is distressing to hear Aikins recalling an abuse victim who said her pastor had told her "this was her lot in life." Officer Aikins stated that in all her experience of domestic violence cases, "I never had one woman tell me that she had a pastor or someone in her parish that she could turn to for help." That reinforced Aikins's own experience: "When I was going through the worst

85

of the problems on the night shift . . . I did *not* have a pastor I could go to. . . . There was no way I would have taken my concerns to that priest." Church leaders, clergy, and counselors create their own world, which they communicate clearly through verbal and nonverbal messages. That world might be one of compassion and care, or it might be one of denial of any problems in the parish; it might be one of anti-woman sentiment, or it might be one of support and encouragement. The church world then creates itself because people who have problems will not discuss their lives with leaders who have communicated a stance of denial or of being unsupportive— leaving church leaders with the erroneous assumption that there are no such problems in their parish.

Officer Aikins went through much of her career doing her job without much reflection on the presence of God in her work world. Only when she was faced with crises did she stop to reflect on the fact that God must have been with her all the time. This realization has enriched her spiritual life, and she will probably continue to reflect on the presence of God in her work environment. Healthy spirituality does need regular reflection on the relationship between the individual and God, including the relationship that occurs on the job.

Each of us needs to reflect regularly on where and when God has been active in our work. This reflection brings us closer to God and helps us appreciate the presence of God on a daily basis. God does care about everyone at all times—not only about those in church on Sunday.

It is always a temptation to segregate our thinking about God and to conceive of God only in terms of church activities. Law enforcement officers may tend to dismiss the many good deeds they do every day because they are done in the official capacity of the government rather than under the auspices of the church. If God were to be present only in the person of the clergy, or only in the name of the church, much of the good that is done by Christian people in our society would be left undone, simply because members of the clergy do not necessarily come in contact with the most needy people or the most critical situations. People first call the police—not the church—when rape, theft, violence, murder, assault, and other offenses occur. People first call the sheriff or the state patrol— not the church—when tragic traffic accidents happen. They call law enforcement officers first when children disappear, or when spouses become violent. Yet all of these things have devastating effects on the spirits of the people involved, including the law enforcement officers themselves. There needs to be a partnership between law enforcement officers and church leaders, between church institutions and state agencies, so that the full humanity of all the people involved can best be served.

•6•

KENN ZIEBELL

I'm Being Punished

Suicide and its tragic effects

Sergeant Kenn Ziebell is a late-shift supervisor in District 7 of the Milwaukee Police Department. Sgt. Ziebell had faced about everything an officer could face. He handled it well, but then he faced suicide. He tells us what it is like to face death when it hits an officer where it hurts most, in his own family. Sgt. Ziebell's story is an inspiring one in which he turns aside from his own suffering to reach out to help others in similar situations. He has been a leader in the organization Survivors Helping Survivors. Sgt. Ziebell is Lutheran.

On November 18, 1984, my oldest son, Tom; my youngest son, Mike; myself; and another man and his son all went to a Green Bay Packer game. That was always a big thing for us, the Packer game. The game was excellent. We had a real good time that day. After I dropped off the other man and his son, I talked to my two boys. I said, "Your mom may ask about going out to eat tonight. Would you mind if just she and I went alone? I'd like to talk with her." My wife was having an affair, and I had filed for divorce. The boys said, "No, no.

We understand. No problem." I said, "OK. I appreciate it." Otherwise, they always went out with us. We always did things as a family.

When we got home, it was around five-thirty in the afternoon. Tom called his girlfriend. When he hung up the phone, he said, "Can you believe it, Dad? She's still in her nightgown! At five-thirty in the afternoon!" A few minutes later he said, "I think I'm going to run over there." I said, "Well, if she's in her nightgown, I don't know if I want you going over there." He laughed and said, "Dad, she could be naked and nothing would happen!" I said, "All right. You just go and behave yourself." I mean, he was eighteen years old.

So he left, and from what we found out later on, he spent the evening there with her and her parents. Her father's a firefighter. Her mother uses a wheelchair. They all spent the evening watching videotapes. Then the parents retired.

We found out later on that while Tom and Laurie were sitting on the couch she told Tom that if he went into the air force, she was not going to wait for him. Well, he was between a rock and a hard place. He had already enlisted, and he had to go.

There was a knock at the patio doors. She excused herself and went to answer it, saying, "I'll be right back." Evidently he checked out there later on and saw her kissing a boy that her parents forbade her to see. With that, Tom left their house.

He came home, and he must have gone right into his room, where he wrote a note. Then he went back into the garage. It's not attached to the house. He barricaded the door, put a hose from the exhaust pipe into the car, and started the engine.

When I got up in the morning, I noticed his bed hadn't been slept in, yet the door opener for the garage was on the table. I pushed it to see if the car was in there, and the door wouldn't go up. I just got a gut feeling right then. I ran into the bedroom and I slipped on some pants and a sweater. As soon as I got to the garage, I could hear the car running.

I forced the door open. Tom was sitting upright behind the wheel of the car. I'm quite sure that when I pulled him out he was already dead. I yelled for my wife to call the fire department. Then my youngest boy came along. I didn't want him to see Tom like that, so I told him to go down to the end of the driveway and watch for the fire trucks. I did CPR on Tom until they got there.

Then, of course, the police were called. When they got there, the fire lieutenant and the police sergeant on the scene were arguing in our kitchen about who was in charge of this crime scene. The police officers and the sergeant all knew me, but I didn't think they should be arguing like that in front of my family in those circumstances.

The fire department was extremely helpful. They worked on Tom for a long time, although I think they knew it was futile. When it was time for them to go, the paramedics came to my wife and me and asked, "Would you like to have a few minutes with him?" I wasn't able to do that, but I thought it was pretty decent that they would allow it. Sometimes we cops get too caught up in the rules. "You can't touch this, you can't touch that, you can't do this, you can't do that," because of all our training about preserving the evidence and respecting the law. With the paramedics, the situation was handled very personally. This was our firstborn son. They let his mother have a few minutes with him. That sticks in my mind as a positive thing, something that I would want to do for other people.

•

When we arranged for the funeral, one of the things that my pastor told us was that he didn't want to glorify Tom's suicide so that other kids would think it's the proper thing to do. They might think, "I'll get this recognition if I kill myself," or "I'll be a hero," or "They'll all be talking about me if I kill myself."

I agreed that we should not glorify suicide, but at the same time I felt that Tom had not been given any real recognition for all the good he had done in his life. He was being shunned. I guess that the word "commit" suicide means you are doing something wrong anyhow. The word "commit" sounds negative to begin with. So maybe that's the way people really do look at it, that it's a terrible thing to do.

I had real jumbled-up feelings about the funeral. On the one hand, I would have liked to have had a real nice burial service for Tom. On the other hand, I had heard somewhere that you can't go to heaven if you commit suicide, that you're not welcome in God's kingdom. So I had second thoughts about asking the pastor if we could have a church service, because I was afraid of getting a lecture or of it being confirmed that Tom couldn't go to heaven. I didn't want to hear that, so I avoided it. I said, "We'd just like to have a service at the funeral home." To this day, I really don't know what that pastor's views are on it.

I've heard other people from our suicide survivors support group who tell us stories about how their priest or church would not conduct a burial service because the person had committed suicide. Some of these experiences happened years ago. Maybe it is different now. But it was one of my fears that I would hear the wrong things from the church. So we just had a simple service at the funeral home.

•

Tom had already bought Christmas gifts for his mother and me, and he had told me what he was planning to buy for his brother. So we bought what he would have purchased for his brother, and we all opened his gifts to us weeks after he died.

That Christmas, I kept referring to myself as being like a deer that was gutted out, because I felt that empty. Christmas was a month and one week after Tom's suicide. I don't have much enthusiasm for Christmas anymore. I don't look forward to it. Putting up lights or a tree or decorations doesn't excite me. It used to be a big thing.

When the suicide happened, I was on the board of elders at our local church. I felt like I was being punished by God. I felt like I'd been doing things wrong and now I was paying for it. It angered me because I thought, "If I'm being punished as far as the divorce goes, and my wife doesn't want to be with me anymore, fine. But to punish me with my son's death, that is too much."

As the divorce proceedings went on and it was finalized, I was doing my share of drinking and just horsing around, not really caring much about anything. I felt that I was not living up to what an elder should be, so I resigned from the board. The pastor and the head of the elders sent me a letter saying my name had been put back in nomination, but I wrote them back saying that I just didn't feel that the way I was living my life right now was appropriate for a leader in the church.

I never blamed God for my son's death. I'm not against him for anything that has happened. It's just that I felt at the time that I was being punished for something.

•

When my son committed suicide, I was on the tactical squad in the department. They've got a reputation for being tough, hard-core, macho guys. I got sick of that attitude a lot of times. In fact, that is why I left it, because if you didn't come across as being real tough and aggressive, you were nothing.

I'll tell you some experiences that made me go against their type of thinking. You can't turn to anyone for help when you are on the tac squad. If you do, you're a wimp. If you're involved in a shooting, the guys come up and pat you on the back and say, "Hey! Nice job! Nice job!" I don't think they mean that they are happy that you blew somebody away. They are just saying, "Nice job, you're still alive." What happens is that if the officer is having problems with the shooting, he's afraid to turn to anybody, because if he shows that it is affecting him, he's not "one of the guys." Well, I was having some real difficult times, because I needed to talk about some things. Divorce is one topic guys can talk about, because everybody hates the ex. They can relate to that. "She deserves everything you can stick her with," and all that stuff. You can talk about divorce, have some drinks, and get over that. But about any other incident? You're supposed to have a hard shell and not say anything about it.

So, during that period of time, I didn't have anyone to turn to except my partner. Not only would he let me talk a lot about my son's death and the divorce, but he would ask questions. That was really helpful, because it was a place where I could relieve that pressure. In addition to my squad partner, I talked to my brother who is also a police officer, but I think I burned him out. I noticed real quickly that I could slip things into the conversation and he wouldn't even know it. For example, we could be talking at night, and all of a sudden I could say, "The sun is shining real bright," and he'd say, "Yeah." He wouldn't even hear me. So, that ended my conversations with him. But my partner was real helpful. We had been partners for such a long time. I first met him in 1975, and we had a lot of things in common as far as families go.

•

The big help for me (I'm talking of the suicide now) is the group Survivors Helping Survivors. The way I found out about it was through the fire department that responded to our home when Tom killed himself. One of the paramedics there called St. Luke's Hospital and gave our name and phone number to them. I got a call from them, they sent literature to our house and invited us to their December meeting.

That first meeting we went as a family. A friend of Tom's came along. I was just amazed at how many families were there. So many people have had the experience of suicide in their families!

Tom died just three days before Thanksgiving. There was a family at that meeting whose relative had killed himself after that time, so they were even newer than we were. Just listening to them, I started to understand that everything I was feeling inside, someone else was feeling also. Some were even hurting more than I was.

We went to a few meetings, and then my wife wouldn't go anymore, so I kind of backed off, too. I was wrestling with a lot of problems. I found myself drinking more and more to escape. I didn't drink at home, but I would go out. It would be an excuse to go out. I drank a lot of beer to forget everything.

Somehow I got back into the suicide survivors group. The more meetings I went to, the better I could handle the pain. While I was working with the survivors group, some of the other people must have seen something that I didn't see, and they asked if I'd be interested in becoming a facilitator. I went to a workshop and was trained as a facilitator. I began facilitating one of the groups sponsored by the hospital and then started going around talking to different police departments.

First of all, we made a tape for the Milwaukee Police Department. It was just a one-on-one interview. It was seen by everyone in our police department from the chief on down. At our in-service training, every officer in the department saw it. Making the tape wasn't difficult, but watching it played back was real hard. I wasn't looking for nice comments, but I got a lot of them from other officers. I was amazed at how many came up and said they had a relative who had killed himself—their father, their brother, a nephew, or someone else. I never realized before how many people are killing themselves.

Out of the information on the tape, some cards were developed containing information about suicide counseling. Every police officer was issued one. The cards are laminated so that cops could carry them around with them. When they got to a suicide scene, they could follow the card while they talked to the family and asked them, "Would you be open to someone giving you a call regarding this suicide?" Such help is not forced on anybody. Survivors Helping Survivors does not go out and solicit people. They do not call up the police department and say, "Did you have any suicides today?" It's strictly based on someone relaying the information that a family would like to be contacted.

I have been part of a panel that talked to the Milwaukee County Funeral Directors Association. We related these ideas to them so that when they are approached by the family of a suicide victim they have another resource to offer the family, to help them in their grieving. We've spoken to numerous police departments and to paramedic personnel and to social service groups at hospitals.

•

There is a terrible, terrible amount of guilt involved with suicide, whether it's rightful guilt or wrongful guilt. That's the hardest thing for the survivors to deal with. It wasn't until January of last year that I finally understood that my son had been thinking of suicide for months before he did it. I had never realized that before. It turned out that he had written notes to his girlfriend's sister, telling her that he was thinking of suicide. I found her responding notes in his room recently. She told him, "I don't like it when you talk about suicide." The notes were dated six months before he killed himself.

Tom never said a word to me about it. I was the one that had talked to him about suicide. I had thought of it myself. See, that's where my guilt was. I felt I had planted the seed in Tom's mind. I can remember one day when my two sons and I were having a discussion about their mom and me. I told them that I was on the edge of suicide and that I even had gone out into the garage one night thinking of killing myself.

All I can remember Tom saying at that time was, "Why you?" I thought he meant "Why not Mom?" or something. But I understand now what he meant was, "I'm the one that's been thinking about it." I had no idea what his thoughts were at that time. It was over a girlfriend that he killed himself. He left a note for us. I found it in the morning.

•

When I go to police departments I talk about being sensitive at the scene of a suicide. So much good or so much bad can be done in those initial moments. Here are a few examples. If it's a suicide in which a person shoots himself or herself, the officer might ask, "What did you have that gun in the cabinet for?" That's a mistake. Right away it makes it seem like the survivors did something wrong. The guilt was there before the officer even arrived, however. A police officer could add more guilt to it by saying, "What did you have the gun there for?" or "Why didn't you call us?"

Each police department has its own rules and regulations, and I'm not intending to interfere with them. All I'm saying is that cops at a suicide scene should be careful how we word things. We can explain to the people that there are questions we have to ask, but they shouldn't be offended by them or take them personally. And mean that. We shouldn't just say it because it sounds neat, and then in the back of our minds be accusing them of doing something or failing to do something. Our attitude really does set the tone for how quickly or how easily a family recovers.

•

When cops talk about people who have completed a suicide, we say, "Evidently the pain was so bad that they couldn't stand it here." Sometimes I think, I was there myself. I know how I felt. I know that I just didn't care what took place. I really never thought about what the consequences would have been for my kids. I knew that there was insurance money for

97

them, but I didn't think of what it would do to them psychologically. I didn't know about suicide then. I knew of some suicides, but they hadn't affected me or touched my life in a personal way. I really didn't know the *feelings* associated with it. When my son died, however, I saw how it tears the family apart, how it tears individuals apart, and the guilt that is there. I would like to think that I would never put my son, Mike, through that. But there are times when I still feel so low that I say, "If I could just close my eyes and not wake up, fine. Take me that way." If that happened, I wouldn't be disappointed. But if my son knew that I committed suicide, he would just have another terrible burden on his shoulders.

I'm kind of wrestling with this issue again right now. My mother was given some very strong medication. The pharmacist told me, "Don't keep that within reach of the patient, because there will come a point when she is going to be in such pain that she'll say, 'I'll just take too much of this.' " On one hand, I can't blame her. If it happened, I wouldn't hold it against her. On the other hand, I would feel awfully guilty if I picked that medicine up and left it where she could get it. So, I might end up having two suicides on my conscience. Knowing how that would feel to me, I wouldn't do that to my son, either.

•

I've been told that one of my problems is that I blame myself too much for things. I don't blame God for my troubles, but where *is* God in all of this? I don't ever like to say that I doubt God, because I believe there is a God. But there are times when I look at the material part of life rather than the spiritual. If a material thing—a door or window, or whatever— is here today and tomorrow it gets smashed, it just no longer exists. There is nothing that comes from it, or becomes of it, but trash. It's just gone. Sometimes, I think that's as it is with life: We are here for now, but when we close our eyes and we're dead, there is nothing else beyond that. I'm hoping that's wrong, because there are a lot of people I'd like to see after this life and be with.

Still, there are times where I doubt a life hereafter. It goes back to a couple of shootings that I've been at, where we got there just moments after it happened. You know that five minutes ago this person was screaming and yelling and arguing with somebody. Something was going on. And now, there he lies. He's nothing anymore. He's dead. He'll never, ever be here again. You wonder, where has he gone? The *body* is here. Where has *he* gone? All the things he ever did or thought in his mind, do they go somewhere else? Then I say, they couldn't have, he's still here. Maybe we are all being fooled by thinking there is another life somewhere else.

But, then, you see other things as a cop, miracles that happen. Someone that by all rights should have been killed but wasn't. Or a person who was in a severe accident gets out of the car alive, walks up on the highway, and then gets struck by another car and killed. That has happened! You say, "Well, it must have been his time! He cheated death the first time. He thought he was going to walk away, and God said, 'No, you are going to die, and that's it!' " Other miracles will be, for example, a baby who survives that logically shouldn't have, or a person who recovers from some sort of terminal illness and goes on to live for many more years. That kind of makes you think that somebody is watching over us.

I've thought about it myself, too, when I'm out on the street at night. I've wondered how many times I have come close to death. How many times did I just miss being struck by a car or shot or attacked? Is that God watching out for me? I don't know. For every time I think there is no God, something turns me around and makes me believe there is. That's what keeps me on the straight and narrow.

•

I still attend church. Sometimes its difficult, especially at the time of year when they start singing some of the Christmas hymns. Then it's hard. I get a lump in my throat and stay pretty quiet in church. But it gives me a chance to go and ask for forgiveness for what I've been doing lately. So it is still a part of my life. I'm sure it always will be so. I can't just see shutting the door on my religion.

I have kept going over and over in my mind, "Why would God let these tragedies happen?" You hear he is a loving God, and yet accidents happen and tragedies occur. Then it finally dawned on me this past weekend when a little seventeen-month-old boy was abducted and murdered. It finally hit me that no loving God would allow that to happen to a baby—to let that child be tortured. I read the police reports so I know how badly the baby was treated. I can only conclude that God has no control over things like that—what humans do to each other. But he will step in at times of tragedy and help mend the hurts and pain.

I have stopped believing that God causes tragedy or uses it as punishment. After that little boy was so brutally tortured, how could I say he loves the children and then let that happen? I have been told that God suffers as much as we do when such tragedies occur, and he reaches out in love to help us recover. I still wrestle with the question.

Comments by the Authors

Sergeant Ziebell makes a very important point when he says that suicide survivors will recover from the tragedy better if they are treated with respect and sensitivity by the police who arrive on the scene. Law enforcement officers don't always realize the impact they have on people, especially at traumatic events. The survivors will remember for years afterwards how they were treated and what was said. Some remember in great detail the first words of the officers who notified the family of the death. It is important to begin right then to put the family at ease, to dispel the guilt that is inevitable. Training in suicide response and death notification should be available for all officers.

The tough, macho attitude that Sergeant Ziebell experienced in the tactical squad has started to change in departments that have mandatory debriefings after traumatic events. We are seeing a change from the attitude that any officer who is troubled by a shooting, a suicide, or any other event is a "wimp." A department can contract with the local mental health care system to offer critical incident stress debriefings, and departments can develop peer support groups where officers support other officers at the scene of traumatic events. It is vitally important for officers to know what reactions to expect from their bodies, minds, and spirits when they encounter events that trigger strong emotions. Knowing in advance what to expect is the first step in caring for one's health. If you know how your body and mind will react, you can better judge when you need professional help due to overreaction and when you are just going through a stress reaction that is within normal limits.

Law enforcement officers are no strangers to suicide. One person asked poignantly, "How do you reach the officer who is sitting there at home with a Smith and Wesson in one hand and Jack Daniels in the other?" Not only do officers encounter the suicides of others, they also consider it themselves. Ziebell calls our attention to his own temptation to solve his marriage problems in that way. Departments need to be ever vigilant for signs of depression or despair that might lead to suicide. Being macho and never talking about personal or job-related problems sets the stage for using this "ultimate solution." Officers need to see other options besides the "permanent" one. Peer support groups, a mental health program, and/or a chaplaincy program could help officers find ways of dealing with their problems. The opportunity for confidential and personal conversation is crucial to the health of officers. However, if an officer does confide that he or she is considering suicide, even if the conversation is confidential, it should be mandatory that the officer be referred to appropriate authorities, cared for, and personally brought to a mental health facility and that the commanding officer be notified. Suicidal comments must be taken seriously.

The doubt that Sergeant Ziebell expresses regarding an afterlife is natural. We all have doubts at one time or another about God, about life after death, about any number of things. There are contradictory messages coming at us all the time that could be interpreted one way or another. As Ziebell points out, the dead appear so lifeless that it is hard to believe there is a part of them that will live on. It is healthy to acknowledge and evaluate those contradictory messages and observations. It is unhealthy to deny that we have doubts. What is needed is a sympathetic friend to listen with us, a spiritual director if one is available, or a religious friend who could help us sort out the messages. The danger is not in doubting, but in cutting off honest communication with God. That is what stifles spiritual growth.

Ziebell mentions that he never blamed God for his son's death and that he doesn't like to doubt God. Sometimes that kind of attitude blocks, rather than opens up, communication with God. If a person resists being totally honest with God, resists saying to God that he or she *is* blaming God or doubting God, then spiritual growth may be stunted. All relationships have trying times, and the relationships between God and police officers are no different. The solution to such troubling feelings is not to deny them but to bring them out in the open, to wrestle with them in prayer, and to come to some resolution.

Ziebell states, "For every time I think there is no God, something turns me around and makes me believe there is." The something that turns a person around may be called the grace of God. God is always reaching out to us. Sometimes we become aware of that presence but can't explain it. It is more of a feeling than an idea. But God is patient. God lets people take time to think about things, to evaluate in their own way the evidence they see around them. This evidence comes to us not only in the places we expect it—in church or in nature, for example: it also comes in the most unexpected places—at an accident scene or sitting alone in a squad car at midnight. The more we learn to pay attention to those quiet promptings of the heart, the better we are at developing a closer relationship with God. That is, after all, the goal of the spiritual life.

The questions of whether a suicide victim should be buried with a full religious ceremony or whether the victim will be able to enter heaven have gone through an evolution. There was a time when suicide victims were buried outside the cemetery walls, suggesting that they were ostracized in some way. Today, more concern is given to the feelings and rights of the survivors than to the question of the state of the victim's relationship with God or the religious community. Funeral rites of suicide victims take place in church and are treated like those for any other tragic death. Ziebell's fears about a church funeral were based partly on stories he had heard from the past, but he was also hearing contradictory messages from his church. The days following such a tragedy are not times when family members have the most courage or presence of mind. It is most beneficial if clergy or lay ministers would take the initiative to offer information and positive reassurance. Many suicide survivors are timid about asking for such information, and may live for years with outmoded beliefs that hinder their recovery. Pastors need to be sensitive to members' needs.

Sergeant Ziebell has turned around a very traumatic experience in his own life and used it to help others. He helps other officers, agencies, and individuals understand and deal with suicide. His own pain has been part of his life even as he served others to relieve their pain. Such dedication to others is a mark of a spiritually mature person and is an inspiration to the rest of us.

One thing we need to keep in mind is that people contemplating suicide sometimes tell others of their intent. Tom Ziebell had written to a friend, who responded to him in writing, but the friend did not tell a responsible agency or adult about the situation. Sergeant Ziebell himself told his sons that he was contemplating suicide, and even told them how he would do it. The boys worried about this but did not tell anyone. It cannot be stressed strongly enough that suicide messages are serious. Any person who hears such a message, including a police officer, should take immediate action. When a person gives a suicide message, he or she is asking for help. It is not always stated directly, but the attempt to ask for help is there. Only an expert is able to judge whether the threat is genuine, so no message of that kind should be ignored, ridiculed, or minimized.

There are many ways to help both survivors of suicide and those who contemplate suicide. Support groups, newsletters, mental health agencies, community health agencies, and other national and local programs stand ready to offer assistance. Officers and family members need to be aware of all the resources available so they can use the appropriate ones for their situation. Churches are a natural place for such information to be gathered and discussed before the need for it arises. Law enforcement agencies should have training programs in place and policies for their employees to follow.

After this was written, Sergeant Ziebell's other son died. Sergeant Ziebell says that losing both of his children as quickly as he did has left him with a lot of unanswered questions. His mother also died.

•7•

DEAN COLLINS

I Believe in a God Who Loves Us

Law enforcement is doing God's work

Deputy Inspector Dean Collins, commanding officer of the Personnel/Administration Bureau, Milwaukee Police Department, has been a police officer for twenty-three years. His story illustrates some of the dangers and diversity of police work. It also demonstrates a balance of religion and work that has fostered a healthy spirituality. Inspector Collins uses his religious faith for the benefit of others by serving as an ordained deacon in the Roman Catholic Church, by offering prayers and benedictions at public police functions, and by counseling officers. Collins continues to wrestle with the meaning of evil in the world, especially as it involves the work of police officers, who "see evil out of all proportion to its existence in the universe."

I joined the police department on July 7, 1969. At that time I was a student at the University of Wisconsin–Milwaukee, majoring in sociology. I was also a member of the national service fraternity Alpha Phi Omega. Within that fraternity, there was another college student who had joined the Milwaukee Police Department. He was still taking courses part time, but he was a full-time police officer and member of the fraternity. So that piqued the interest of various other fraternity members, including myself. Three of us applied for the police department at the same time, and all three of us were accepted.

At that point in 1969, two years after the riots in Milwaukee, the police department was recruiting heavily for police officers. We had no difficulty being hired on the police force with our college backgrounds.

It was a very turbulent time period, because the Vietnam war was in progress. We found ourselves confronting our own classmates at various demonstrations. We were very young and very eager. Almost every night we ended up piling into patrol wagons with our helmets and our sticks, never knowing where we were going. It was tremendously exciting. There was always that feeling of electricity in the air, the feeling that something big was happening and we were going to be part of it. We policed demonstrations where we were confronting people whom we had known on campus who opposed the war. That was my introduction into police work.

•

My introduction into deeper involvement in my religion, surprisingly, also happened through the police department. When the Second Vatican Council restored the diaconate as a permanent order, it was also reintroduced in the Archdiocese of Milwaukee in 1975. I was not aware of it immediately, but another police officer became a deacon. At that time, it was a very unusual thing. There was a lot of press coverage about this officer, who was an ID technician who took fingerprints and photographs. He and I had worked together on the streets, in uniform, in District 3.

I had read about this guy entering the diaconate, and I became curious. I asked him what the diaconate was all about, what the seminary training was like, and what it was that deacons did. After several of these conversations I wanted to know a little more. I went to orientation sessions with the people who were running the diaconate formation program. Karen, my wife, had to attend these with me, because you can't enter the training in the seminary, much less be ordained, without the consent of your wife.

The more I thought about the diaconate, the more I was drawn to it, and I applied for admission. I looked at the application for the entrance into the seminary, and it was much, much longer and much more detailed than the one I filled out to become a police officer. They required all sorts of references. I had to write my autobiography and send a picture. It was very thorough, very detailed. Then I was given the MMPI (Minnesota Multiphasic Personality Inventory) test, and various psychological tests. I had an interview with a clinical psychologist to go over the results of those tests. Finally, the admissions board made the decision whether or not I would be accepted, which I was in 1981.

I think the thing that attracted me most to the diaconate was the very essence of the diaconate, which is *diakonia*: service. I believe it's not unusual for police officers to go into the diaconate. There is one other who was ordained with me, and I've heard of more than a few in Chicago, in Los Angeles, and other places. I think that says something about police work and it says something about the diaconate. There is this very strong attraction to the service ideal, both in law enforcement and in the diaconate.

Law enforcement, at least traditionally, looked upon itself as very close to the ministerial priesthood, or to the ministry. It required the same kind of selfless dedication of being on call twenty-four hours a day, dealing with matters of life and death, being able to keep confidential some very sensitive and potentially damaging information about people.

From an altruistic standpoint, law enforcement means to be of service to others, to be a servant, as in the long-standing term *public servant*. Law enforcement has, for a long time, had this service ethic—"to serve and protect."

The diaconate was restored to fulfill the ancient hierarchy of the church, which has always included deacons. It was restored, not just for a liturgical purpose, but to have certain people as the living sacramental sign of the church's service in the world. The work in the world that many of these Christians were doing would be strengthened by the sacramental grace of Holy Orders. I see a very strong connection between the secular police profession and the clerical calling as a deacon.

•

I went to Catholic grade schools, and then went to Marquette University High School, and graduated in '65. All through that educational experience, there were classes in religion. Having the Jesuits as teachers was a good experience for me. But I didn't have any inclination to become a priest.

In fact, my faith life just kind of drifted along as most other people's seem to do. At some point after I became a cop, I stopped going to Mass. I was not practicing my faith for three or four years, until the time when I decided to get married. That was an obvious time to reassess my faith life, in terms of whether or not we were going to get married in a church. After talking about it, we discovered there was no doubt in my mind or in Karen's mind that we would get married in a church.

So I came back to the church; I realized that it offered something very important that had been lacking in my life. I started going back to Mass and became much more interested in my faith. I became active in my parish, and when we bought our current home I joined a parish nearby. I became the director for the lector program and also for the eucharistic ministry program. So I had some involvement with the church before I entered the seminary.

I felt a very strong attraction to the diaconate, but it is hard to really put my finger on it. I wasn't struck by a bolt of lightning on the road to Damascus. It was just a very persistent, a very strong attraction that led me to take that step.

Of course, it is the church's responsibility, duty, and right to test such calls, to determine whether or not they are authentic and whether or not they are calls that the church should honor.

I wasn't sure whether or not they were going to take me into the diaconate, because I had been involved in a shooting. One of the impediments to ordination, and there are a whole series of them, is that one cannot have committed homicide. So I didn't know what they would think about my having killed someone. I told them the whole story. It was in the papers and on TV. There was no way I could hide it, and it never entered my mind to hide it. I wanted to lay everything out there and let it be strictly in God's hands. I found out that the canon, as it defines homicide, is really more akin to willful murder, and that self-defense either as a law enforcement officer or as a member of the military has never been a bar to ordination. And so I was accepted in the seminary and after three years of study was ordained a deacon on June 9, 1984.

•

The service ethic which has been the motto of police departments everywhere, "to serve and protect," is the unselfish giving of one's self for others. Being a law enforcement officer gives an average Christian layperson a unique opportunity to be of service. Even on a purely secular plane, we are being of service, doing God's work, as is mentioned in Romans 13 and various other passages. When we also bring to that work a spiritual motivation, it is truly God's work. This is not the same thing as wearing our religion on our sleeve or talking about it all the time. Our faith becomes evident in our willingness to be of assistance, to help other people, to go out of our way for the good of someone else.

People recognize that motivation in our work as law enforcement officers. We're not just doing it because we're paid to do it, or because it's a job like any other job. People can discern whether or not an officer is really interested in them and their problems. We can just go through the motions, but that's readily apparent to people. When we take the time, and we really care about them, it shows. I think most people recognize that kind of compassion, that kind of concern, is more than just a secular concern. It has happened many times, especially with family troubles, and in times of grief, and tragedy, and sorrow, where coppers have gone that extra mile. People have noticed, have felt the difference, and commented on it. They write letters of appreciation to the commanding officers and to the chief because people felt an officer's compassion.

•

In thinking back over my career, I ask myself what stands out in my mind after twenty-three years of police experience. I think it is a sense of duty. I think back to the very earliest days when I was walking a beat. That is an experience that most officers don't have anymore. I recall being a rookie, being out there alone. That was the era before everybody had a handy talkie radio that they could clip on their belt. I remember walking in some of the really bad areas in the middle of the ghetto and being the only one out there, answerable to myself alone, in a sense. There was nobody there, no partner, no radio that I could use to call for backup. Walking, walking, walking. Walking for almost eight hours each night.

I was afraid. I think every rookie is afraid until they make the first couple of arrests. Then they realize, "Hey, I can really do this! I can arrest people! Most of these people will submit to my authority. I won't have to fight all of them." It is winning the first few fights that gives you the confidence you need to really be a good law enforcement officer.

There were so many experiences, but they have kind of dimmed through the years. Every officer keeps a memo book, though. Those memo books go back to the beginning. Every single day is recorded in them.

I can remember going on a call in 1969 when we used to have the ambulance service. One of the first ambulance conveyances I made was with a veteran copper. He drove the ambulance, and I was the attendant. We got sent to pick up a dead person relatively close to the station. It was in the afternoon. It was a warm spring day. We were directed to the backyard by an hysterical woman. And there, lying in his garden, was an old man, face down, wearing a faded light blue shirt. We gently turned him over, and then we noticed where the police department patch on his shirt used to be. This was an old, retired copper. He had died of a heart attack in his garden. We picked him up on the stretcher and put him inside the ambulance. We went to the morgue to get him "pronounced." On the way to the morgue, I was sitting in the back with him. I was looking at his face. He was thin. Kind of lanky. He had white hair. I thought to myself, "God, is this how I will end up someday? Will some snot-nosed rookie be looking in my face, in the dead face of a retired copper wearing an old police shirt?"

•

Law enforcement is an almost universal profession. It is the same all over the world. I watched a documentary on the militia in Russia—that's what the police were called in the former Soviet Union, the militia. This hour-long documentary showed them doing basically the same kind of work we do, in uniform. These weren't KGB agents. There were no spies. This was basic law enforcement. A stabbing, an auto theft, punk rockers, a motorcycle gang. You wouldn't believe that these things even existed in the Soviet Union. We were so used to thinking that it was a police state, that they had everybody under a system of repression. It's not so. I looked at this documentary and said, "My God! They could work here and we could work there, if we could only speak the languages."

Law enforcement has a privileged, unique view into human nature, into human existence, that nobody else has—not even the clergy. We see, we hear, we experience those things that doctors and lawyers and supreme court justices and psychologists and psychotherapists only deal with after the fact, in a very sterile and civilized environment. We are *there*. We are privy to all sorts of things newspaper reporters never hear about.

Take, for example, the vice squad raids that take down an escort service. We get their entire computer file. We know all the customers! We know all the clergy who've been arrested for child abuse. We know all about the politicians and lawyers who beat their wives. We know a lot that most people never hear about. We not only hear about it, we experience it. We participate in it. That's why we can be amazed and puzzled and angry and even amused when we read newspaper accounts of events we actually experienced and say, "It never happened that way at all. They've got it all wrong." We were there. We know what happened.

•

As with many officers, I was involved in a shooting. At the time it occurred, and even today, I felt a very strong need to talk about it because there are things about the event that are mysteries. If one thing had happened, as opposed to another, the results would have been different. If I had not responded to the backup call or if we had fallen back and taken up a perimeter position rather than going in, for example, the entire outcome might have been different. The man I killed, a twenty-four-year-old Vietnam veteran, might be alive today.

The shooting happened on April 8, 1975. I was working in District 4 and was a sergeant at the time. On occasion, the sergeants would go out plainclothes to monitor the response time of our uniformed squads. So I drew a squad car—a "plain-clothes car"—from the headquarters garage. Normally, I would have taken a car out of the district station lot, but since the purpose was to catch officers unaware, I drew a car from the central garage downtown. I remember asking the garage sergeant to give me a car that had a shotgun in it. Most of the squad cars had shotguns, but some of them didn't. I always said to give me a car that had a shotgun in it.

I took the car out, and it was around eleven o'clock at night. The shift started at midnight. I was in the district and driving around, ready for hitches to go over, so I could see how long it took the officers to respond to each call. Around two-thirty in the morning I heard a call for backup for a squad facing a man with a gun on 40th and Silver Spring, which is one of the main arterials in Milwaukee. I was already eastbound on Silver Spring, at about 37th Street. Since I was in plain-clothes, in an unmarked car, no one knew where I was. I could very easily have kept driving east until I got to Lake Michigan. No one ever would have known. I could have just kept on going and never answered the radio, and no one ever would have found out. But morally I could not do that. If an officer is in trouble, when that call comes over you go no matter what and as fast as you can, because you know another officer is probably fighting for his or her life.

I turned my car around and parked on Silver Spring, in the middle of the street. One of the officers motioned for me to come over and very briefly told me what happened. This two-officer squad made a traffic stop at Teutonia and Florist. As they were booking the driver for a speeding violation, the passenger got out of the car and the driver took off. Well, the officers still had his driver's license. They said, "This is no big deal. We know where he lives." They finished writing the ticket, and they went up to his house on 40th and Silver Spring. They knocked on the back door, and they saw him coming to the door with a shotgun. That's the point at which they called for an assist.

They quickly related this to me while we were in the dark, at about 2:30 A.M. At that point, one of the officers stayed at the back door, and I went back to my squad car, which was in front of the house. All of a sudden, the guy came out of the front door, onto the front porch, with the shotgun pointing at me. I was in the street behind my unmarked squad. My shotgun was out. I jacked a round into the chamber. I took deliberate aim at him on the front porch. My finger was on the trigger and I was about to squeeze it, when all of a sudden one of the officers leaped onto the porch and grabbed the suspect's shotgun by the barrel.

I left my position and started running around my car on Silver Spring, to come up to the porch. By the time I rounded my squad car, the other officer had managed to grab the shotgun from the suspect and throw it over the porch onto the front lawn. At that point, the suspect ran around the officer, and went directly into the house.

So now the suspect was inside, and all three of us followed him into his completely dark house. Help was already on the way. The tactical squad had been called, but at that point the only tac squad in the city was on the south side. We were on the far, far northwest side.

The suspect ran through the house, to the back of the house, where there was a kitchen. By this time, the father of the suspect came on the scene, and he was totally intoxicated. The suspect shouted out, "Don't come in here! I've got a gun! I've got a gun!" We were thinking, "Wait a minute. The gun he had was thrown over the porch railing." But he insisted he had a gun. "Don't come in! Don't come in! I'm going to shoot you! I'm going to shoot."

We were all standing by the doorway trying to see into this completely dark kitchen. I was at the doorway, and behind me were two, by now three, officers. One officer was on his stomach, flashing his flashlight into the interior of this darkened kitchen. The father said, "Don't shoot my son! He doesn't have any gun!" The son says, "I've got a gun! If you come in here I'm going to shoot you." The father said, "Well, if you've got a gun, point in the air and shoot it." We were saying, "No. No." All of a sudden, "Kabooom!" He had a gun.

What he did was fire a 30-caliber deer rifle through the ceiling of the kitchen, through the second floor, through the attic, and out through the roof. We shouted repeatedly to him,

"Put the gun down! Come out. We're not going to hurt you."
He said, "No, no. Get out of here. I'm going to shoot. I'm going to shoot."

I was at the threshold of the kitchen. There was no door there. My shotgun was pointed into the room, but I couldn't see anything. Before he fired the shot, a spot of light was dancing all over the room as the officer on his stomach was trying to stick his flashlight into the kitchen. In that fleeting light, I caught the muzzle of his gun. Instantly I knew what kind of weapon he had. He had a lever-action deer rifle. So after he fired the shot I waited, because I knew what was coming next. I'm waiting. Is he going to jack another round into the chamber? Sure enough, he did. At that point, I knew I was going to have to shoot him.

Almost immediately after he jacked another round into the chamber I could see the muzzle, and that's when I fired. When I shot, his arm was up and his weapon was pointed at me. I fired at him with a regulation police shotgun, which was a Remington 870, carrying a 00 Magnum Buck load. The distance from me to him was probably ten feet. The entire shot pattern caught him underneath the armpit and traveled completely through his chest cavity and just shredded his heart.

It was a big explosion in a very small kitchen. He went down with my shot still ringing in our ears. We found the lights, and there he was, lying on the kitchen floor. The father was going berserk. We had to get him out of the house. I immediately cranked another round into my shotgun. That's the training. You don't presume that the person is dead. Many times they're not dead.

But there was really no doubt in our minds this time. We went on the air and called for an ambulance. We called for a detective bureau squad. I called my lieutenant, saying, "I'm at this address, 40th and Silver Spring, and I just shot a guy." His first comment was, "Are you OK?" This concern for one another in police work has been there for a long time. We just haven't promoted it or cultivated it, or even said much about it. But at the time it felt very reassuring.

At that point, we had to secure the scene. While we were waiting for the detectives, the pool of blood in the kitchen was getting bigger and bigger and bigger, because there was a direct hole from his heart, through his chest, to his armpit, from which all his blood was seeping across the kitchen floor. While we were waiting there, a black cat came downstairs, walked over across the kitchen floor, and started to lap up the blood. We grabbed the cat and locked it in a bedroom. I'll never forget that as long as I live.

•

What really happened is that the suspect used me to help him commit suicide. We did not know it at the time, but we subsequently determined that he had fired other shots inside the house before we arrived. He was wearing army dress greens, in the pockets of which were over twenty rounds of shotgun ammunition. He had left a note, something about Vietnam and about dying, and it had suicidal qualities about it. He refused to put the gun down. He refused many commands, many pleas, "We don't want to shoot you. Drop the gun. Drop the gun."

Only after it was all over did we discover all of these things. His blood alcohol level was about .24—twice the legal limit for intoxication. The whole thing said to me that he used me to help him commit suicide. There have been many cases where armed suspects have provoked officers into killing them. They gave the police officer no choice, really, by making a threatening move with their weapon. So it's not unknown that these things happen, but you sometimes don't realize it until it's all over.

The next morning I had to call my wife and tell her what had occurred. She was very shaken by it. I was in the D.A.'s office. We have a different procedure today, but then I was the suspect. It was the strangest feeling in the world. I didn't know whether I should remain silent, invoke my Miranda rights, or what. I was very much alone. I knew that I had done the only thing I could do, because if the man had fired, the slug would have gone through me, and through the officers who were standing behind me. There is no doubt in my mind what the result would have been.

If I had just kept on going east on Silver Spring that night, I would not, today, have this eternal link or relationship to the dead man. Had this person not bumped past the other officer after being disarmed on the front porch, he'd be alive today. On the other hand, suppose that we had waited for the tac squad. The man had the shotgun, and he had twenty rounds of ammunition. He could have started a real fire fight from that residence on that corner of 40th and Silver Spring.

What if he had not had the deer rifle in the kitchen? Or what would have happened if he had just put the gun down? Or what would have happened if I had frozen at the last moment and said, "I can't shoot another human being!" Such questions live in the mind of every officer that goes through a shooting. What if something different had happened? What if one of the variables—the time, the location, the meshing of persons and places—had been different? Would I be alive? Would the suspect still be alive? You don't know. But you never stop thinking about those "what if" questions.

•

The man was buried from a church in the district. I was very curious. I wanted to go to the funeral. He was so much a part of my life and he would be forever. Not just until I die, but even into eternity. Someday I may meet him again. I don't know if he was morally culpable for what he did, or what he forced me to do to him. I can't be his judge. But for the rest of my life, I am related to him in a very special way. I *killed* another human being.

117

I wanted to see what was going to happen at the funeral. Were there people there who would mourn him? Did he have a family? Did he have a wife? (I found out later he was single.) What did they think? What did his relatives, his family, his friends think about what happened? But I did not go. In a sense, I felt guilty. It would seem almost insulting if I were to be there, as if I had a lot of guts, or no shame. I felt that the family would be deeply offended if I had gone to that funeral.

At one point I felt very angry that this man did this to me. Yet, as the years went by, I couldn't continue to blame him. I think that he was in real pain. I think he was suffering from something, something very deep. He was intoxicated. I don't know what was in his mind. I think about the Christian ethic of forgiveness, I think of the Vietnam post-traumatic incident syndrome, and I find there are a lot of reasons why I don't blame him anymore.

No officer who kills another human being will ever forget it. I don't dwell on it. I don't think about it on a regular basis, but once in a while something will happen to bring back the memories. There will be a shooting incident and it will trigger my own. Whenever I hear that an officer has shot someone, it all comes back to me.

•

I think the reason our officers become cynical is that they have never pondered or dealt with the question of evil in the world. Evil is a mystery. It remains a mystery, like God's grace remains a mystery. Why does one plane fall out of the sky and another doesn't? Why are certain passengers on a train killed and others survive? We live in mystery. But the police, by their unique calling, are enmeshed in pain and suffering and evil. That's what makes their job so difficult. They see evil out of all proportion to its existence in the universe. It seems the only things they see that are good are within their own families, and even then they have their own family problems.

118

People don't call the police for good things. They call when something bad is happening. Some of these are really very traumatic events. People tend to look upon the police as somehow beyond human consideration, that somehow we are a different species, a different breed, in that these things should not or do not affect us. In point of fact, they *do* affect us. We have children. We have parents. We have relatives and friends. Very often, we see our own flesh and blood in the place of that particular victim, especially in cases of sexual assault, extreme brutality, homicide.

I don't think law enforcement as a profession has pondered the significance of those experiences. We have not examined the mystery of evil in the universe or in our own profession. I like Rabbi Kushner's approach in *When Good Things Happen to Bad People* (New York: Avon Books, 1983) that sometimes things happen for no reason at all, that there are random events in the universe, that there was no grand plan or design behind certain events, that God does not will evil things to happen in the world.

We live in an imperfect world, a world that is governed by physical laws—laws of gravity, laws of chemistry, laws of physics. Wings fall off of airplanes, metal fatigue causes bridges to collapse. An aircraft crashing nose-down allows some people in the tail to survive. These are things that I don't think God can be blamed for, although the people who are in very great pain as a result of the death of a loved one naturally blame God because they believe that God is in control of everything.

Kushner's hypothesis is, "Not necessarily so." God is active in the world. God has not abandoned us. Miracles still happen. But at the same time, God does not suspend the laws of nature to save individuals on a routine basis. If he did, the chaos which he dealt with at the beginning of creation would again collapse in upon the universe.

I believe in a God who does not cause evil or pain or suffering. I believe in a God who created the world as a good

119

place and who, out of simple justice, could not let the sin of Adam and Eve—however one conceives of that—to go unpunished. I believe in a God of love, a God of mercy, a God of compassion, a God who died on a cross for us. I believe in a God who suffers with us, who commiserates, who has compassion with us in our sufferings. I cannot believe in a God who hates us enough to inflict these tragedies on us.

It is natural for us to blame God, to curse God, to rail and rant and rave and scream to heaven as Job did. If that makes people feel better, that's fine. God can take it. As we mature in our faith lives, however, we can grow beyond those feelings of pain and anger and realize that God didn't cause bad things to happen. Suffering is the result of living in a sinful world, a world that is not heaven. Pain happens to everyone, in one way or another. But we are not alone in our pain. God feels our suffering along with us.

It is the job of pastoral ministry to make people understand that they are not alone in their pain and their suffering. That is where law enforcement comes in also—to bring some measure of comfort, to bring some sympathetic presence. Pastoral ministry is being present, suffering with, sympathizing with, another person who is suffering. To the extent that law enforcement officers can do that, and we can, we are just as important as a priest, deacon, or minister would be.

Comments by the Authors

Deputy Inspector Collins has shared the philosophy with which he approaches his work in the police department. He says, "I see my law enforcement profession, which is my secular profession, and my ordained profession as being one and the same." That profession is one of service to others. Collins's philosophy might easily be dismissed by some officers, who could say, "I'm not ordained, so that doesn't apply to me," or "I try to keep my private life (religion) separate from my public life (work)," or "That is mixing church and state, which is not allowed." However, church and state are already mixed inside every officer who works for the city, county, or state government and is also a member of a religious denomination. To separate the two is to become internally torn apart, to be divided against one's own self. A person's integrity requires that there not be major contradictions between the philosophy that undergirds his or her spiritual life and his or her professional work.

While not many law enforcement officers are ordained as clergy, many are baptized or dedicated to a religious tradition as members of a particular religious denomination. This commitment to a faith tradition serves as an ethical foundation for their work as officers, although some people may not know how to take full advantage of their own spiritual heritage. Of course, police departments would not want their officers to go around preaching to or proselytizing their fellow officers or the public, but they do want morally upright officers who are mature and secure in their relationship to God and to others.

The movements in Collins' life into the police department, back into the church, and into the diaconate were all spurred by the influence of friends: a friend who entered the police force and encouraged others to follow; a fiancee who discussed their marriage in a church context; a friend who entered the diaconate and who, by his public example, encouraged Collins to do the same. God often speaks to us through our friends or others. We need to be open to hearing new and different directions pointed out to us through these very familiar accents and not minimize the importance of friendly voices in our journey through life.

Collins experienced no radical conversions, just the gentle pull of an example here, an attraction there, to which he responded after asking a few additional questions independently. The initial reasons for entering the police department, the church, and the diaconate turned out to be simply beginning points. After entry, however, Collins discovered within himself deeper resources that helped build a career, maintain church membership and a relationship with God, and sustain the work of the diaconate.

While Collins mentions keeping record books of every single day of his law enforcement career, he does not mention keeping a formal record of his religious career. Journaling, the daily recording of our faith experiences and relationship with God, is a good way to judge where our faith journey is leading us and to evaluate whether we are healthy in mind, body, and soul. Police officers might be surprised to learn things about themselves that their own journal would reveal, such as repetitive habits, commendable practices taken for granted, the gentle presence of God's grace in their lives. Our religious lives are at least as important as our secular lives and deserve at least as much attention. We are asked to account for our secular lives daily. Should we not also account to God and to ourselves for our spiritual lives on a regular basis?

Deputy Inspector Collins mentions prayer several times in the story of his career. He uses prayer in several ways: as part of liturgical functions such as funerals and weddings; as a way to relieve stress; as a petition to God on behalf of a dead suspect; in praise, confession, supplication, and thanksgiving that are assumed by Collins's role as deacon in the Mass. No doubt he also prayed for his own safety on occasion.

Prayer is a way of connecting ourselves with God, of giving balance and meaning to our lives, and of tying up the ragged ends of such events as the untimely death of a fellow officer or suspect. Sometimes silent, sometimes vocal, sometimes brief, sometimes long, sometimes happy, sometimes agonizing, prayer can be as natural as breathing and as life-giving as breath itself. Prayer is not something that should be left to the clergy but is something that every person has to do for himself or herself. Prayer is an intimate lifeline to God. It is the first line of defense against tension, despair, fear, and spiritual disintegration.

Police officers, Collins points out, come face to face with evil every day. They confront evil "out of all proportion to its existence in the universe." Reflection on the relationship between good and evil is traditionally done by theologians and religious professionals. Most such people, however, do not encounter the level of evil and violence that law enforcement officers do. A clearer understanding of evil would be found if conversations were held between priests and police, between theologians and law enforcement professionals. Officers would do everyone a favor if they would initiate such conversations with their religious leaders.

The development of their spiritual life helps law enforcement officers deal with the serious challenges that face them every day: not only the challenges of violence and injustice, but also the challenges of mystery, both the mystery of evil and the mystery of God's grace.

Law enforcement officers do in a physical way what priests and other clergy do in a spiritual sense: they save people, they comfort people, they bring justice and peace to society, and they do so with care and confidentiality twenty-four hours a day. Yet the physical and the spiritual aspects of life cannot be so neatly separated. Both body and spirit are intimately intertwined. Both aspects are ministered to by both the police and the clergy in their everyday contacts.

• CONCLUSION •

The police officers interviewed for this book have shown that, within the same occupation, the way each one approaches the job and his or her own spirituality varies with each individual officer. Nevertheless, all of them have grown increasingly healthier and closer to God as they moved through their careers in law enforcement.

We wish to thank each of the officers who have generously shared their time and their stories to make this book possible. In so doing, they have helped many other officers who may be struggling with similar questions.

In response to the needs and challenges expressed in this book, a group of law enforcement officers, including some whose stories appear in this book, have been instrumental in creating an organization called the Law Enforcement Assistance Network, Inc. (LEAN), which offers conferences, training, and retreats for law enforcement officers. This organization is a nonprofit corporation that exists to help police officers develop their personal, ethical, spiritual, and professional lives. A percentage of the royalties from the sale of this book will be donated to LEAN for the benefit of law enforcement officers.

We urge all of those interested in pursuing the ideas and issues presented in this book to contact us at the address below.

Law Enforcement Assistance Network
3316 S. 84th Street
Milwaukee, WI 53227
Chief David Steingraber, President
Dr. Judith Kowalski, Executive Director